RUTH SLAVID

MICRO
VERY SMALL ARCHITECTURE

LAURENCE KING

First published in Great Britain
in 2007

This paperback edition first
published in 2009 by
Laurence King Publishing Ltd
361–373 City Road
London EC1V 1LR
Tel: +44 (0)20 7841 6900
enquiries@laurenceking.com
www.laurenceking.com

Text © Ruth Slavid 2007
This book was produced by
Laurence King Publishing Ltd

A catalogue record for this
book is available from the
British Library.

ISBN-13: 978-1-85669-594-7

Designed by Hybrid (London)

Printed in China

RUTH SLAVID

MICRO

VERY SMALL ARCHITECTURE

LAURENCE KING PUBLISHING

CONTENTS

INTRODUCTION

Opposite: Thorncrown Chapel, Eureka Springs, Arkansas, E. Fay Jones, 1980. This much loved building embodies, on a larger scale, many of the main attributes of microarchitecture.

In the year 2000, members of the American Institute of Architects voted, in a spirit of millennial enthusiasm, for the ten structures that they considered the best to have been built in the twentieth-century. Number four on this list was Thorncrown Chapel, designed by E. Fay Jones and completed in 1980. It was not a complex structure, but a single space, constructed from timber and fully glazed, set in the woods near Eureka Springs, Arkansas. Built up from small structural members that could be carried by hand, it was constructed without the need to cut down any trees. In 1981, *Newsweek* described it as 'metaphysical', and it has been loved, admired and well used ever since. Thorncrown Chapel is 18.25 metres (60 feet) long, 7.5 metres (24 feet) wide and a soaring 15 metres (48 feet) high, an admirable set of proportions that make it rather large in terms of the projects described in this book. But compared to many ecclesiastical buildings, it

deserves the epithet 'tiny' and it shares many of the properties that can make small projects such a joy.

First is simplicity. Structurally, Thorncrown is extremely sophisticated, but that sophistication goes towards the creation of a single beautiful space. By eschewing complexity, architects can keep a sense of total control. There are few major projects that can be seen as entirely flawless, however magnificent the overall achievement. It is rare for an architect to complete a large building and feel satisfaction with every detail.

Scale down again from Thorncrown and the possibility of perfection is even greater. Microarchitecture means to me the construction of really tiny spaces, of buildings that are more like artefacts. Often but not always they have just a single space. It is relatively easy to consider them as a whole, to transfer from drawing or rendering to the real thing, without any horrible surprises. Not all the

buildings here are precious – some are deliberately rough and ready – but they are all somehow considered, since a single jarring element could ruin the whole conception. Few strive for greatness, but several are as good as they possibly could be.

Other elements that these tiny structures share with their larger brother Thorncrown include a pleasure in the use of materials. The environmental concerns of E. Fay Jones (very impressive in 1980) not to damage the building's surroundings are common although not universal, as is the ability of these buildings to punch above their weight in terms of the impact they have, in both atmosphere and appearance, and sometimes also in importance.

So what is microarchitecture? I have deliberately avoided defining it by a specific floor area. It is to me simply the architecture of the really small, of the building that either serves a single function, or does something more complex

in an unexpectedly small space. A house so small that bedroom, bathroom and kitchen rotate in turn, to be tucked away when not needed? That's microarchitecture. A small structure that serves just one function, such as a sauna house? That's microarchitecture. A tiny bandstand on wheels that can be rolled away, a seaside shelter that spins with the wind, a temporary lookout on top of a solid Tuscan mansion? Microarchitecture, all of them.

One of the advantages of these projects is that they are often within the scope of young architects. Many cut their teeth on interiors, fitting out bars and shops where they don't have to be trusted with tricky things like keeping the rain out or getting the plumbing right, but that is not the most satisfying way to work. Fit-outs are often ephemeral, dependent on fashion and restricted by the structure into which they are inserted.

A really small but complete project, however, offers the gratification of producing something that is all one's own. It does not depend on the ability to assemble and manage a large team, to call in the specialist advisers, or to satisfy the requirements of a complex programme. Rather like the sample works that some apprentices produced to show that they had completed their training, a piece of microarchitecture can be a tour de force that proves an architect's mettle early in their career. They may even be able to finance it themselves.

One person who is keen to promote this kind of achievement is architect and academic Richard Horden. Although certainly not a new starter (he was born in 1944) his constant inventiveness has run alongside work with students, encouraging them to stretch their imaginations. Since 1996 he has been professor at the University of Technology in Munich, Germany, where he founded the Microarchitecture Unit Munich. It is through the investigations with his students and in collaboration

with German firm Haack + Höpfner that the micro-compact home (m-ch) has evolved (see page 136), the first of Horden's long line of fascinating projects that is likely to go into large-scale production imminently.

Horden's definition of microarchitecture concerns not only scale but also lightness. 'Our own definition of the term,' he wrote in *Detail*, December 2004, 'refers to objects that are lifted physically off the ground and only minimally in touch with it, "touching the earth lightly". It also involves a search for new typologies … in which we seek to achieve and experience more with less. We aim to minimize the use of materials and energy, to integrate transport and habitation, while creating a tighter fit between architecture and product design.'

This approach has resulted in such iconic projects as the triangular car-top cabin, the helicopter-shaped Ski Haus that is in turn lifted into place by helicopter, and the improbably slender and elegant Beach Point

lookout. All use extreme economy of materials, relying on technology to provide the strength that previously would have come from large sections. 'Reducing dimensions,' Horden wrote in the same article, 'has the effect of reducing the quantities of materials used, the energy consumed in their production and transport, the amount of material required physically to support this process, and the energy needed to heat and cool the interior space.'

The only architect who could make Horden's work look a little heavy is Frenchman Gilles Ebersolt who, alongside some more prosaic work, has devoted the major part of his practice to what he terms 'architecture *hors sol*' (architecture above ground), floating structures that allow scientists to investigate the natural world way above ground level. Horden may describe his designs as 'touching the earth lightly', but Ebersolt's often don't touch it at all (see page 90). It is interesting to see the way that this level of invention can then translate into

more grounded projects, such as creating extra space in a photographer's studio (see page 212).

To get to the remote places for which they are designed, Horden and Ebersolt's creations have to be both prefabricated (at least in part) and transportable. These are two traits that run in parallel alongside microarchitecture. Almost all the projects in this book are prefabricated to some extent and many of them are portable in the sense that they will spend their lives in many different locations.

Portability is, of course, limited by size, but prefabrication is not the sole prerogative of very small buildings, since it is possible to build up larger structures from smaller, ready-made elements. It is an ethos increasingly embraced by industrialized countries, keen to get away from the messiness and uncertainty of construction sites. In the UK, for instance, the government has been promoting for several years the concept of Modern

Below: The Ski Haus in
Switzerland, designed by
Richard Horden Associates
in 1991, was one of the key
pieces in the development
of lightweight, transportable
microarchitecture.

Methods of Construction
(basically any kind of offsite
manufacture) alongside the
idea of the £60,000 house,
an inexpensive (and hence
compact) housing design
that was the subject of a
competition that reached its
climax in 2006.

Portability is linked to the
idea of rootlessness, either
forced as in the case of
refugees and jobseekers
or voluntary in the case
of those who have made a
conscious decision not to be
tied down.

The Office of Mobile
Design, based in Venice,
California, describes its
approach like this: 'By
designing non-permanently
sited structures that move
across and rest lightly upon
the land, OMD is rethinking
and re-establishing methods
of building that contrast
with the generic clutter
that increasingly crowds
the landscape. Inspired by
Sant'Elia's Futurist manifesto, OMD shares the philosophy that 'we no longer
believe in the monumental,
the heavy and static, and
have enriched our sensibili-
ties with a taste for lightness,
transience and practicality.'

All the designers discussed
above are architects, but
not all the projects in this
book were generated by
architects. That is a reflection of both the relative
simplicity of the projects and
of the conceptual nature
of some of the designs.
There is a blurring both
between microarchitecture
and product design, and
between microarchitecture
and art. This is apparent
in projects such as Simon
Starling's *ShedBoatShed*,
which won him the Turner
Prize (Britain's top art prize)
in 2005. Starling bought a
shed, which he turned into
a boat that he paddled down
the Rhine to Basel, where he
rebuilt it into a shed. Erwin
Wurm's Fat House, first
shown at ArtBasel in 2004,
sits beneath a conventional
pitched roof, looking as if
the walls have exploded into
an orgy of lard.

Subversion of the shed is
not restricted to fine artists.
The 'Ideal Hut Show' in
Glasgow in 1999 asked people as diverse as architect
Ian Ritchie and fashion
guru Paul Smith to take a
basic garden shed and per-
sonalize it. So successful was
the concept that it migrated
to the Métis garden festival
in Quebec in 2002, where
ten Canadian designers un-
dertook a similar exercise.
London's Victoria & Albert
Museum then followed suit
with ten artists in 2005.

Below left: Fat House by Erwin Wurm, first shown at ArtBasel 2004, is an excellent demonstration of blurring the boundaries between architecture and art.

Below right : Bulging Room, Alison Scott, 2002. Designed by University of Manitoba architecture student Scott and exhibited at the Métis garden festival in Quebec, the Spandex walls of the shed allow more and more objects to be crammed in – a comment on modern consumerism.

When artists and architects coincide there is inevitably a playfulness that neither may achieve on their own. Tiny projects are similarly light in conception if not always in weight. You can achieve a lot with a very small building, but pomposity and portentousness are, thank goodness, almost always out of reach. So however serious the very diverse projects in this book may be, they are also all fun and entertaining. Microarchitecture, among its other strengths, will, if it is any good, bring a smile to the face.

PUBLIC REALM

Facing page: Public lava-
tory and flower kiosk, Westbourne Grove, London,
UK, CZWG, 1990s.

Below from left to right:
Late nineteeth-century pho-
tograph by Eugène Atget
showing a Parisian street
complete with distinctive
vespasiennes.

The grand, glass-domed
underground lavatory at
Macquarie Place, Sydney,
Australia, shown in a photo-
graph taken in the 1930s.

Public lavatory, Groningen,
the Netherlands, Rem Koolhaas, 1996. The opaque
glass lavatory is fun but has
to close in winter due to
danger of freezing.

The architecture of our public realm is usually only considered by default. Get it right and nobody notices, but get it wrong and there is either an outcry or a feeling that the environment has been degraded without knowing why. If this is true of the more minor elements of street furniture – the litterbins and the posts that support an unnecessary panoply of signs – it is even truer of the major incursions on our streets – the public toilets and bus shelters.

The concept of the public lavatory in the West took off in the nineteenth century, in Paris with the highly decorative street-corner pissoirs called *vespasiennes* after the pioneering sanita-

tion work of the Roman emperor Vespasian and also in other major cities. Campaigns towards the end of that century ensured that there were facilities not only for men but also for women, allowing them to venture confidently beyond the confines of their homes.

Outside Europe, one city that built rather grand public lavatories was Sydney, Australia, with, for example, a grandiose glass dome signalling an underground lavatory at Macquarie Place. Even after the facility itself was filled in, the dome was retained as a feature.

By the end of the twentieth century, the trend in public lavatories was towards the

installation of the self-clean-ing Sanisette, a practical approach with no distin-guishing design features. Instead, its selling point was that it was freestanding, self-cleaning, secure and did not require staffing.

Despite the often inglorious history of public lavato-ries, some architects have turned their attention to their design. For instance, superstar Rem Koolhaas designed a public lavatory in Groningen, the Nether-lands, in 1996 that is clad in opaque glass decorated with lively photography by Dutch photographer Erwin Olaf. Another photographer, Ivar Hagendoom, has described it as 'fun, albeit slightly dys-functional. The drain that

you can make out in the front right of the picture appears to be for both water and urine, so to get in and out you have either to step across or wade through.' This is a definite triumph of form over function, as the lavatory has to close in win-ter as it is likely to freeze.

Equally eye-catching but rather more successful is a combined lavatory and flower shop designed by Piers Gough of CZWG in the 1990s for Westbourne Grove, west London, which created a distinctive coloured landmark on a tri-angular piece of pavement.

Japanese architect Shuhei Endo (whose Rooftecture S appears on page 162),

Below left: Shuhei Endo's Springtecture H public lavatory in Shingo-cho, Hyogo Prefecture, Japan. Built in 1998, it is part of his series of buildings using curved corrugated metal to give dignity to mundane building types.

Below right: Eisenman Architects tackled the challenge of the bus shelter by designing the outsize Angle Pose for Aachen, Germany, in 1996. Local reaction to the 'giant crab' was mixed.

designed public lavatories in Hyogo, Japan in 1998 as part of his Rooftecture series of buildings, using curved corrugated metal, that also included bicycle shelters, another important piece of the public realm. More recently he has designed others, using weathering steel and with a more sober appearance.

Bus shelters have been another Cinderella area of design, compared not only to conventional buildings but also to other types of transport building. International superstar architects are proud to turn their hands to railway stations, and some also become involved with underground railways. The city of Bilbao was so enamoured of the perky entrances that Norman Foster designed for its metro that it dubbed them 'Fosteritos', and many architects who are now part of the British establishment were given a boost by designing stations for London Underground's Jubilee Line extension.

Even bus stations and garages have a more illustrious history than the shelter, with, for example, the magnificent concrete structure of Stockwell bus garage in south London, designed by George Adie and Frederick Button and opened in 1953. In 2000, a bus station in Walsall, in England's Midlands, opened to great publicity. Designed by London-based practice Allford Hall Monaghan Morris, it was a key part of the regeneration of this run-down town, which also included an award-winning art gallery by Caruso St John. And multi-disciplinary practice Arup designed a somewhat clunky but definitely eye-catching bus station in an attempt to knit together an urban jungle at Vauxhall, south London, in 2005. All this is on a larger scale and also more of a one-off than the humble bus shelter, with its associations of teenage trysts, graffiti, urination and simple dis-piriting waiting. American deconstructivist Peter Eisenman designed a bus shelter called Angle Pose for the central plaza of Aachen, Germany, to mixed reactions, with some disgruntled residents referring to it as a 'giant crab'. And it is the word giant that is key, since this was far beyond the size of a conventional shelter. Similarly, the decision by the city of Anchorage in Alaska to spend $1.5 million on a bus shelter outside its new Museum of History and Art has led to an outcry over the extravagance. Even the bus and tram shelter that Santiago Calatrava designed in St Gallen, Switzerland, in 1996, which has an elegant

Below left: Santiago Calatrava's Bohl bus and tram shelter, at St Gallen in Switzerland, was also way beyond the usual size. It was completed in 1996.

Below right: View of a kiosk from *Atlas du Comte du Nord,* pen and ink and watercolour on paper, 1784, by Chambre. Such ornate follies and pavilions, originally designed for private parks, provided the template for public-park pavilions a century later.

steel-ribbed roof, is way beyond the normal size, as if such architects cannot quite engage with the mundanity of the standard bus shelter.

But there has to be a way of making ordinary bus shelters more appealing, and it is the ability to achieve this that has resulted in so much publicity accruing to Bauman Lyons' series of bus shelters in Bradford (see page 26). By addressing both comfort (heated seats) and entertainment (music) these are, indeed, exemplars of improvement to the public realm.

Australian architect Sean Godsell, however, has a more subversive approach. As a contrast to the exquisite homes he designs for the wealthy, he has addressed the question of homelessness, offering solutions to improve the conditions in those traditional magnets to the rough sleeper, the bus shelter and the park (see page 30).

In most ways, however, parks and promenades are in stark contrast to the other venues considered in this chapter. Whereas bus shelters and public lavatories serve a necessary function, the park and the promenade are intended for pleasure and leisure. This hedonistic role gives more freedom to the architect, but also presents a new set of problems. The golden age of park buildings was the end of the nineteenth century, when, in the aftermath of the industrial revolution, there was recognition that the working public needed places to relax. Some pavilions built at that time borrowed from the vernacular of earlier private parks, as shown in exquisite French drawings by the likes of George-Louis Lerouge, Louis Audot, Pierre Boitard and Victor Petit, illustrating an article by French professor Michel Vernes in the journal *Architecture Intérieure Crée* (no. 320, June-July-August 2005).

Another approach came from embracing the new technology of wrought iron for bandstands, benches and shelters.

For architects in the twenty-first century, the challenge lies in finding a way to create this sense of leisure and pleasure in a contemporary idiom, a task to which the projects illustrated in this chapter have risen admirably.

Nenad Fabijanić
Dubrovnik, Croatia

PUBLIC TOILET

There is a temptation when architects design public lavatories to make them 'fun' places, to install a little toilet humour of their own. But Croatian architect and university professor Nenad Fabijanić has not taken this approach with the lavatories designed for the historic city of Dubrovnik, Croatia. Instead, he has used the same attention to materials and consideration of spaces that he employed on more 'serious' projects, such as the Catholic church in Tivat. The result is a dignified building that sits well in its surroundings, providing facilities that are needed by the growing number of visitors, without cluttering the streets with unsympathetic tat.

Set in the harbour area, just outside the city walls, this building leans against the port authority building. Part of the brief was that it should create a new public walkway between that building and the city wall, and the site constraints meant that it had to be long and thin. Materials also had to be in keeping with the surroundings. The exterior is therefore of local Dalmatian limestone, which has a pale but warm colour. But whereas on the city walls this is used in small, rough-hewn blocks, on the lavatory building the architect has used larger, smoothly faced blocks for a more modern finish. With only a very small offset between the courses, this is evidently a contemporary cladding solution, rather than a structural use of the material. Although the interior plan is a long rectangle, there are opposing angled 'prows' on the ends, creating a more dynamic urban intervention, and channelling pedestrians. On one of the prows, a scoop has been cut out of one of the triangular blocks, one of the few playful elements on the scheme. Entrances are set along the long wall, as are two niches with drinking fountains.

Internally, the walls are clad with black stone, and doors and fittings are of stainless steel – a solution that is relatively vandal-proof while still signalling a commitment to quality. Two domed skylights enhance the natural lighting.

The external paving is also in smooth-cut limestone, at a smaller scale than the cladding, and simple circular uplights are set into it to ensure that this does not become a dark alley at night.

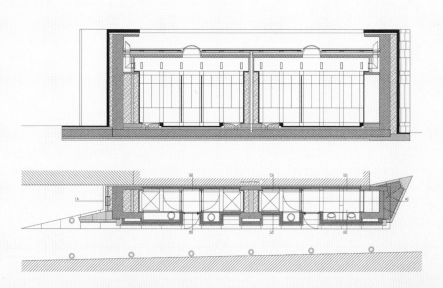

Opposite: Plan and section of the building, showing the cubicles arranged in a straight line.

Left: The sculptural 'prow' of the building signals the presence of something out of the ordinary.

Opposite: The smooth-
faced blocks used for
cladding contrast with the
more rugged nature of the
city walls.

Below: A simple but care-
fully considered lighting
scheme ensures that this
does not become a threat-
eningly dark alley at night.

TOILET BLOCK

Richmond, Tasmania is 24 kilometres (15 miles) from the capital Hobart and is known as the best-preserved Georgian village in Australia. As a result, it has a growing tourist industry, bringing the dilemma that these tourists need the very facilities that could spoil the ambience that draws them there.

The municipal authority, Clarence City Council, therefore thought hard about the best solution. It appointed 1+2 Architecture to design both a pair of bus shelters and a public lavatory that would take coaches away from the historic hub of Bridge Street. The solution is an elegant and dignified one that avoids the pastiche to which so many other buildings in the area have fallen prey, while respecting historic materials.

The project is not just a small-scale piece of architecture, but also involves some well-considered town planning. The three buildings, with similar dimensions and roofs, slide past each other on not quite parallel axes, making reference to the street plan beyond. They stand on an area of simple grey paving.

Although the materials are of high quality, the most immediate allusion is not to Georgian homes but to local farm architecture, in the pitched corrugated metal roofs. In the case of the bus shelters, this roof is virtually all there is, supported on a simple steel structure and covering some benches and a drinking fountain. The lavatories are more complex, with a proper building beneath the open-gable roof, which has some skylights inserted into it. Nevertheless, there is still open ventilation, through a gap between the roof and the tops of the walls.

There are four men's, four women's and one disabled lavatory arranged in a straight line, to one side of a circulation corridor, with washbasins on the other side. Construction materials are concrete blocks, which echo the Georgian ashlar buildings, and horizontal-running oiled eucalyptus.

In general, safety, durability and resistance to vandalism have been priorities, with the lavatory fittings themselves in steel, and with concealed cisterns. This seems to have paid off everywhere except with the timber cladding, which almost immediately attracted graffiti and name carving.

Nevertheless, these handsome structures, part of a strategy to accommodate visitors more intelligently, are an ornament to Richmond when they could all too easily have been a blight.

Below: The spare and
contemporary aesthetic
contrasts with the town's
historic ambience.

Opposite: Pitched corrugated metal roofs, echoing farm buildings, combine with concrete blocks and oiled eucalyptus.

Below: The bus shelters have the same structural form and roof as the public lavatories, but with uninterrupted space beneath the roof.

Bottom: Site plan showing the relationship between the buildings.

1: shelter;
2: public lavatory;
3: disabled lavatory

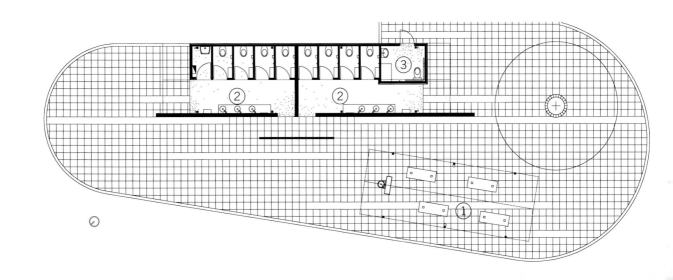

BUS SHELTERS

The city of Bradford, in northern England, embraced the theory that buildings designed with respect are likely to receive respect, and commissioned Bauman Lyons Architects to design a series of six shelters on its new 'guided bus' system. The guided bus, a variant on the tram, is a method of giving public vehicular transport its own acknowledged place in a city. Although it harks back to an earlier idea, it is an essential part of any 'modern' transport system.

In the years in which London's double-decker Routemaster buses, now sadly vanished, and their successors became iconic images of the city, red has been the colour most strongly associated with buses in the public imagination. Bradford's buses have a different livery, but the shelters themselves are in that colour. Although evidently related, constructed from folded steel and glass, the shelters are not all the same.

Two have tall masts with wind turbines on the top generating electricity that is used to heat the seats – a welcome intervention since winters in the north of England can feel bitter. In two of the shelters, artist grouping Greyworld created a sound installation that plays music in response to the colours worn by passers-by, and in another there is a rolling digital display of text that lasts 24 hours on one cycle, providing distraction for the waiting public. Bradford commissioned the shelters as part of its unsuccessful bid to become European City of Culture 2008, ending up with the benefit although not the prize.

In the local newspaper the *Yorkshire Post*, Irena Bauman of Bauman Lyons wrote on 17 February 2004 about the importance of having good clients. 'They are few and far between and we have had the privilege to be commissioned by some of them,' she wrote. 'All in their different ways have taken a risk in order to achieve aspirations above the ordinary with everyday projects.' For the thousands travelling to work by bus, their day should start in a more cheerful manner through having used a bus shelter that makes them feel that they are not just cogs in a system but people deserving of proper treatment.

Previous page: Two of the shelters have wind turbines that generate electricity to heat the seats.

Opposite: The brightly coloured shelters form a key part of Bradford's 'guided bus' system.

Below: Long section and cross-section through one of the shelters.

Bottom: Although all the shelters are slightly different, they have a common vocabulary that makes them instantly recognizable.

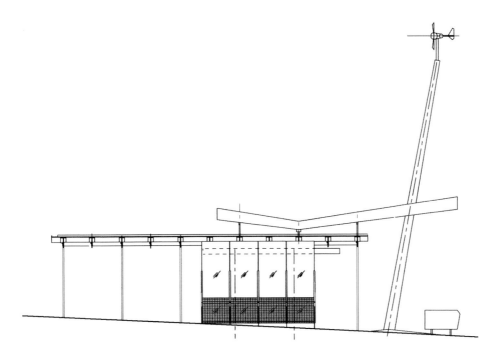

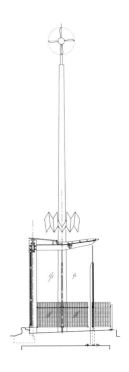

PROJECTS FOR THE HOMELESS

Design one-off houses in beautiful spots and you are, by definition, designing for the rich. So it is to the credit of Australian architect Sean Godsell, who has designed some of the most beautiful and restrained houses, that in parallel he has been addressing issues of homelessness through three projects.

The earliest, called Future Shack, is a way of using 6-metre (20-foot) containers to create dignified living accommodation for the homeless, and particularly for victims of disasters.

Containers have often been colonized on an ad-hoc basis, but Godsell's cleverness lies in making them feel and look like real homes, while still capable of being erected in 24 hours. He built his prototype behind a light-industrial unit in Flemington, Melbourne but such was the aesthetic appeal that reviewers in publications such as *Architecture Australia* immediately started fantasizing about having one on their own patch of land. Part of this

comes from the simple device of having an overhanging roof. Supported on a steel frame that fixes to the outside of the container, this can then be clad in any local material.

Accommodating this exo-structure has resulted in the need for some adjustments to the container itself. The other major change is that the end now hinges up like a garage door to create an entrance, reached by a ramp. This ramp, shaded by the open door above, then doubles as a veranda. Internally, there are minimal divisions and a plywood finish, into which elements such as beds and a table fold away to make the most of the space. Skylights for ventilation have been cut into the roof, and the overall thermal insulation level is good.

Everything that is needed to erect the shack packs away into the container, making transport easy. This includes the supporting structure and the structure for the roof, plus solar panels and water tanks. It is

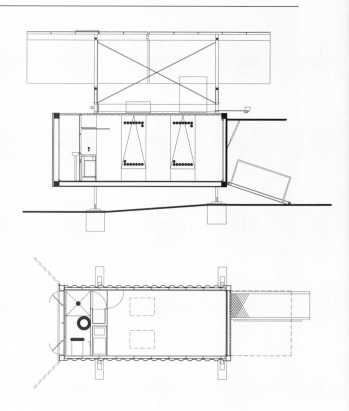

Opposite: Section and plan of Future Shack, showing the overhanging 'garage door' providing shelter to the ramp area.

This page: Adapted from a shipping container, Future Shack has an overhanging roof that both provides shade and gives it more presence.

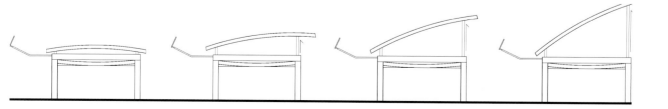

Opposite top left: Finishes inside the Future Shack are simple but stylish.

Opposite top right: Roof-lights enhance the environ-ment.

Opposite below: The open-ing mechanism for the Park Bench House.

Below: A comfortable seat by day, the bench opens up to provide a snug place to sleep at night.

supported on telescoping legs, which can deal with a slope of up to 45 degrees. As the number of people displaced by disaster and war seems to increase every year, so does the relevance of projects like Future Shack. But there are other people who either cannot or will not aspire to such a permanent condition. These are the urban home-less, given a choice between unsavoury hostels, if they can find a place, or sleeping where they can. Godsell has addressed their needs in two prototype projects.

One of these is the Park Bench House, which goes directly against current

thinking that tries, wher-ever possible, to prevent the homeless sleeping on benches. Godsell, aware that his home city of Melbourne has up to 600 people sleeping rough every night, tackled this issue from an opposite point of view. What if you created somewhere that was nice for people to sleep in, which could be restored to normal use during the day, and cleaned easily? His solution was an oversized metal bench that opens like a clam in the evening to accommodate sleepers between its two leaves.

It would be the role of council workers to 'open

up' these beds at night, re-vealing the wire bed-frames. There is even a night-light shining on the ground to signal occupation. It is certainly a more civilized solution than sleeping in a damp shop-doorway.

Again, Godsell developed this as a prototype, and there are still problems to overcome, as the bench probably needs to be larger than envisaged to accom-modate the less agile.

The third of his solutions centres round that other magnet for the homeless, the bus shelter. His idea is that, with a little creative thinking, this could serve

a double function, looking after travellers by day and sheltering the homeless by night. The freestand-ing advertising hoarding at the end of the shelter would be adapted to act as a dispenser of blankets, food and water, and the seat would fold up to reveal a bed. In a third function it could also be used to display artworks. Godsell also envis-ages the glass wall and roof of his shelter finding use as a digital display screen.

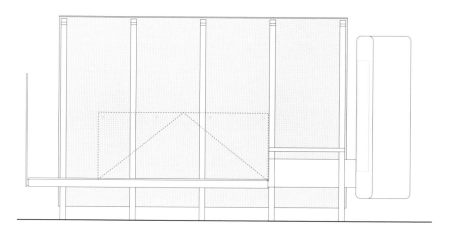

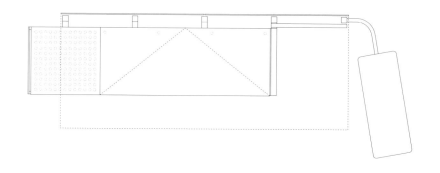

HDW INFO PAVILION

Light and cheerful are the adjectives one first thinks of in association with this little tunnel of a pavilion that hunches up like a caterpillar, lifting itself off the ground on minimal legs. But while the effect may be playful, and all the better for it, there is some serious calculation underlying it, as befits a building produced as a research exercise in a university department. The students who designed the pavilion for Helsinki Design Week 2005, Teemu Seppänen and Antti Lehto, were working in the Wood-Glass Studio at Helsinki University of Technology, Finland. Not surprisingly, wood and glass are the primary elements of the structure, backed up with some carbon-fibre ropes for pre-stressing, and simple L-shaped steel supports.

Counter-intuitively, it is the glass that provides the load-bearing structure, with the plywood enclosing the glass preventing it buckling. The collection of 135 birchwood triangles containing the glass is in turn held within four bows of laminated plywood. Two of these form the end arches and the other two make up the two lower edges, themselves shallow asymmetric arches. The students used a combination of 3-D modelling and small-scale physical models to create the form, which had to be sufficiently curved to achieve stability. Part of the trick in such designs is then to translate those three-dimensional forms into elements that can be laid out flat.

Although the large plywood elements were made in a factory, the students were responsible for all aspects of the design, including programming the numerically controlled cutting machines. The plywood elements were varnished, and the glass was tempered and laminated. A clear glass is used for the outer surface, with a satin-like glass below it, giving the structure a certain opacity.

The students assembled the structure in their workshop, including a lower 'stiffening frame' to hold it all together during construction. One of the constraints was that the pavilion had to be small enough to be transferred to site in one piece.

It was installed in Ateneum Park, just opposite the main railway station. Surrounding it, for design week, was a 'balloon forest' created by students at the University of Art and Design, Helsinki. During Design Week, the pavilion was used to dispense information during the day, while in the evenings similar information was reflected onto the white balls of the balloons. But in addition to their functional roles, the combination of pavilion and forest uplifted a relatively staid space.

In the daytime, the pavilion was slightly mysterious, as its glazed panels reflected the surroundings. At night, lit from within, it glowed like a Japanese paper lantern, informing passers-by that this was a place where they could not only update themselves about what was going on, but also admire the ingenuity that had gone into creating such a playful little structure.

Below: Plywood and glass are the main components of this charming structure, which found a home near Helsinki's main railway station.

Below: During Helsinki's Design Week, the shelter was surrounded by white balloons onto which information was projected at night.

Opposite: The building is made from 135 glazed birchwood triangles, contained by four laminated-plywood arches

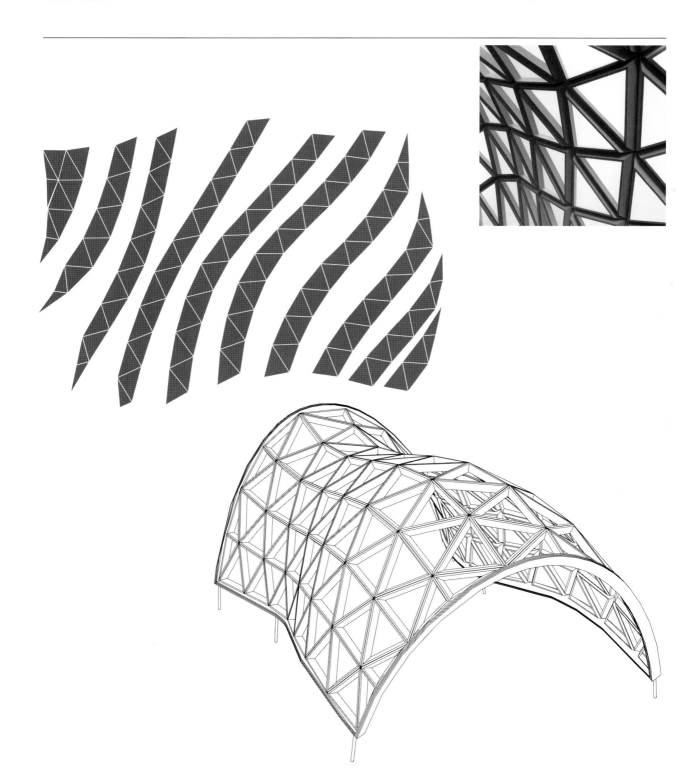

LOOKOUT TOWER

One of the charms of Helsinki, Finland's capital, is that it is situated partly on land and partly on an archipelago of islands within the harbour. On one of these, Korkeasaari, sits Helsinki Zoo, and it was there that the decision was taken to create a lookout, allowing people to enjoy views of the city across the water.

Like the Lilja Chapel (see page 80) and the HDW Info Pavilion (see page 36), the lookout was the result of a student competition for timber design, marrying two of Finland's strengths – wood and education. With at least half of all districts made up of forest, rising to 80 per cent in some parts of the country, timber production is a significant part of Finland's economy. The country also has one of the best educational systems in the world. In 2004 the World Economic Forum identified it as the world's most competitive economy, thanks to its 'culture of education'. These timber competitions, which look for new ways of thinking and carrying the results through into built projects, are an excellent example.

In the case of the lookout, the competition, set by the zoo with Wood Focus Finland, was won by Ville Hara when he was a student at the Wood Studio at Helsinki University of Technology. An open timber framework, with just a staircase, two platforms and some simple mesh balustrading within it, the lookout acts as a sculptural object in the landscape yet allows visitors to enjoy views almost entirely unmediated by the enclosing structure.

Hara's solution was an irr-egular ovoid structure, with a hole at the top and openings for the staircase. It was produced by a combination of computer calculation and trial and error. Over 10 metres (32 feet) high, it consists of 72 long battens, with a section of 60 mm x 60 mm (2 3/8 inches x 2 3/8 inches), that are bent and twisted on the site from seven pre-bent types. More than 600 bolted joints hold the shell structure together. The shape follows the curve of an existing low stone wall, and skirts a birch grove.

Because of the irregularity of the form, Hara found it difficult to draw, so he started with a plasticine model. From digital images of this he created the AutoCAD (computer) drawings and 'taped' the curved battens electronically to form the grid shell. There was also some full-scale testing of pre-curved laminated spruce battens to see if they could be twisted into position successfully. When Hara discovered that they could not, he decided to steam them, a technique traditionally used in boat building.

Eight students erected the lookout over three months. Although it looks delicate, it is structurally very strong. All steel elements have been galvanized and all the timber has been treated with linen oil to withstand the elements. So it should continue to give pleasure for years to come – both to those who spot it from across the harbour and to zoo visitors who want to survey the sea and the city.

Opposite: A simple initial
sketch of Ville Hara's
design.

Below: The lookout sits
on one of the islands of
Helsinki's archipelago,
offering magnificent views
of the city.

Below: Sections through
the tower.

Opposite: When seen by
night, the illuminated form
of the lattice tower appears
more solid.

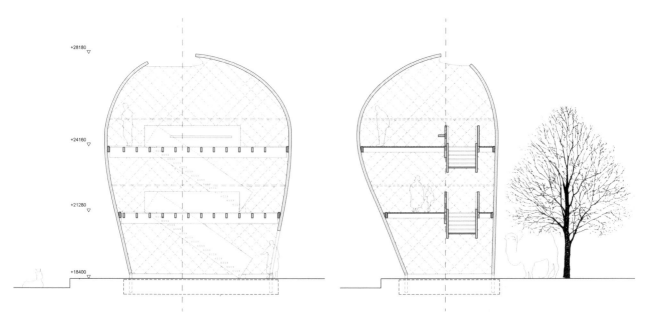

+28180

+24160

+21280

+18400

Opposite: The irregular
ovoid form was refined by a
combination of computer
calculation and old-
fashioned trial and error.

Centre: From inside the
structure, visitors enjoy
almost uninterrupted views.

Below: Straight flights of
timber stairs go up to each
of the two platforms.

OCEAN PARK HATCH SHELL

An enigmatic steel structure has sprung up in the 4-hectare (10-acre) Clover Park in affluent Santa Monica in southern California. It could almost be a distorted climbing frame, if it weren't for the nylon cable threaded through it that makes its elements entirely, and deliberately, inaccessible. Visit it on a still day and you may be confused, but on a breezy day (and the Pacific Ocean brings plenty of welcome cooling breezes to the city) you will hear the wind activating the strings and creating an eerie music.

This is not, of course, a new idea. The Aeolian harp, based on exactly these principles, has been around for centuries (Samuel Taylor Coleridge even wrote a poem about it) and in its more recent manifestations has frequently migrated from the windows of buildings to exposed outdoor locations. But the lack of invention does not reduce its appeal and in this case the structure, the Ocean Park Hatch Shell, has other purposes as well as creating music.

Designed by architect Patrick Tighe of Tighe Architecture, with landscape architect and artist Andy Cao, the Hatch Shell is one of 14 different art commissions for the park since 2001. Described by Tighe as a folly, it can also act as a bandstand or as the backdrop to arts events. It has even been used for a wedding.

The nylon thread does not only add auditory interest. Visually, it creates a kind of misty, interrupted transparency, perhaps reminiscent of the sea mists that afflict Santa Monica on summer mornings. A soft rubber pad inside makes even the act of standing there a slightly disorientating experience. The Hatch Shell is a more playful project than many of Tighe's houses and other buildings across the United States that, while imaginative, have to fulfil practical requirements. But it forms part of the body of work that contributed to Tighe being one of six architects to receive the American Institute of Architects' Young Architects Award in

2006. The jury commented that, 'He is a real talent and it's wonderful to see that his significant work is nationally recognized and varies in type.' Part of that variation lies in designing a folly such as the Hatch Shell, a valuable exercise in freeing the imagination from drainage details and insulation values that can only bring renewed vitality to an architect's other projects.

Below: Patrick Tighe and
Andy Cao designed the
Hatch Shell as one of a
series of art commissions for
the park.

Below: The nylon threads, which vibrate in the wind, also give a misty appearance to the structure.

Opposite: Tighe describes the steel and nylon structure as a folly, but it has also been used as a bandstand and as a backdrop to arts events.

BICYCLE SURVEILLANCE HUT

Scheveningen is the seaside resort attached to The Hague, and has some of the tackiness and fun of a place keen to attract holidaymakers.

It seemed the perfect destination for maverick British architecture practice FAT (the name stands for Fashion Architecture Taste) to create what it determinedly refers to as a 'nonument', a monumental building of minute proportions. The practice members have operated for years like architectural guerrillas, rejecting fashion and taste (and, the more po-faced may say, also rejecting architecture). Finally they are beginning to build some larger-scale projects, both in the UK and the Netherlands, but the little building in Scheveningen is an example of the quirky interventions that have typified their output over the last decade.

Their approach evidently strikes a chord with the Dutch. Not only did FAT win a competition to design the building (too often, they complain, they come sec-ond in competitions, with prospective clients bottling out at the last moment), but at the start of 2006 the building even appeared on a postage stamp. You can't get much more mainstream than that.

On first looking at the 'nonument', you may well ask what it is. Form certainly does not follow function in this instance, but then the function is not known in most countries. It is a bicycle surveillance hut, appropriate to this most bicycle-conscious of countries. People in the Netherlands make 30 per cent of all trips by bicycle, compared to 12 per cent in Germany, five per cent in France and only one per cent in the United States and Canada. But this recognition of the importance of the bicycle does not mean that there is no problem with theft, and that is what the surveillance hut is intended to prevent.

The competition, run by local arts centre Stroom den Haag, sought a design that could be installed during the Fiets & Stal exhibition in 2005. FAT's solution seems to epitomize seaside architecture, looking like something one might discover on one of the more imaginative crazy golf courses. In the shape of a square pyramid – FAT liked the idea of a hill because 'Holland doesn't have any' – it looks white and fairly inscrutable from behind. From the front it resembles a picture-book castle, its steel frame clad in stone, with grey battlements. This folly contains the usual elements – an office, a lavatory, a kitchen and even a loft to store bicycle helmets. Perched on top is a tiny reproduction of a typical Dutch house. At irregular intervals the house hisses and flashes and emits smoke as if it were on fire.

Even in the visually exaggerated world of seaside architecture and folderols, this little building stands out. There is little point in a surveillance building if nobody knows it is there. Having gone from cheeky intervention to, literally, the stamp of authority in just a few months, it can probably expect to morph into a well-loved classic like the most kitsch of American diners. If FAT's ambition is primarily to shock, it has failed at Scheveningen. But its work is likely to raise a smile for years to come.

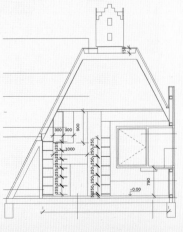

Opposite: Section through the hut.

Top right: Stamp of respectability.

Below left: On one side, the hut presents an uninterrupted solid face, except for the small vision panel halfway up.

Below right: The tiny rooftop representation of a traditional Dutch house is the crowning glory.

BANDSTAND

There is an exuberance to the mobile bandstand that Níall McLaughlin has designed to sit outside the De La Warr pavilion in Bexhill-on-Sea, on the south coast of England, that makes it seem utterly right. So much so, that it is difficult to remember just how wrong this project could have gone. Architecturally, there was a great deal at stake. Bandstands play a key part in the iconography of the fast-vanishing British seaside holiday. One of the most sedate of traditional British seaside pleasures was to listen to a band, often playing military marches, in a bandstand, typically a wrought-iron, circular structure.

This is the function that architect Níall McLaughlin was tasked with reinterpreting at Bexhill-on-Sea. Situated on the south coast, this is one of the least exciting of British seaside towns – with one shining exception. It is home to the De La Warr pavilion, designed in the 1930s by Mendelsohn and Chermayeff, and representing one of the few and best examples of European Modernism of that period to be built in the UK.

A vast ocean liner of a building, intended for public use, it has had a chequered history, although now, happily, it has been restored and revitalized. And the bandstand, once a beacon of optimism and now a sign of success, sits there very happily. Its architect has avoided the twin perils of pastiche and incongruity.

Most bandstands are fixed in place, but the brief at Bexhill was for a bandstand on the expansive south terrace that could be moved around, giving more flexibility. McLaughlin's solution is an airy white structure on splayed spindly legs that has the exuberance of the seaside and the white colour of the pavilion, neither emulating nor battling with the building's architecture.

Formed of plywood ribs and spars that support an outer surface of plywood sheets and a glass-fibre mat, it has a jaunty, wave-like form that grew, not from its surroundings but from the acoustic demands. The architect's original concept, of a simpler shape reminiscent of a megaphone, did not satisfy the acoustic engineer who found that it would have distorted the sound. With the finished design, the combination of convex and concave surfaces means that there are numerous foci for the sound, preventing distortion. The ribs, which are 250 millimetres (9 7/8 inches) deep at the rear, taper to only 75 millimetres (3 inches) at the front, giving the canopy a crisp front edge.

Computer programs were used not only to analyse the form and to design the exact shapes of the ribs, but also then to generate the production information from which the bandstand was made. Although the architect had originally intended to use more advanced materials than plywood, such as steel or carbon-fibre, and was constrained by cost, he has been quoted as saying that: 'Plywood allowed us to deploy traditional joinery skills inventively. It's a common material, with a wonderful strength to weight to cost ratio, capable of magical transformation.'

The shell was made in three parts, as it would not have fitted into a vehicle, or even the contractor's workshop, in one piece. They were brought to site where assembly took only five days.

Steel brackets within the shell are bolted to the steel stand, which can be wheeled around to different fixed positions for different uses. If the wind becomes too high, the bandstand is turned with its back to the wind, so it is less likely to be sent skittering across the terrace. Because the steel legs are splayed, they resist rocking. Between the two front legs is a series of shallow steps, providing both access and an enhanced area for the players to occupy.

With its mobility, the Bexhill bandstand is as much a piece of seaside furniture as architecture. Its cheery profile enhances its surroundings, and is a welcome reminder that the spirit of the British seaside is not yet dead.

Below: Designed to be
moved around for differ-
ent functions, the band-
stand can be turned with
its back to the wind when it
gets too breezy.

Left: Drawings showing the ribs of the structure from in front and from below.

Below left: Sketch model in folded paper.

Below right: Drawing demonstrating how the bandstand was intended to help repopulate the terrace.

Opposite: Two different and complementary kinds of elegance are provided by the new bandstand and the existing De La Warr pavilion.

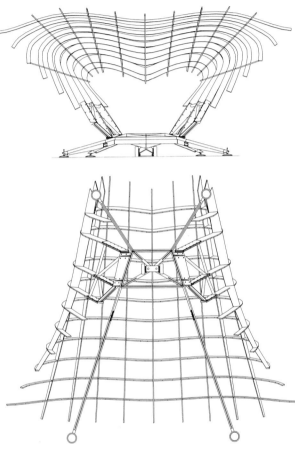

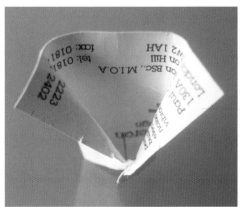

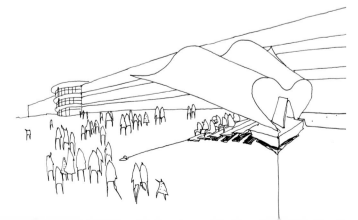

IAN McCHESNEY
BLACKPOOL, UK

ROTATING WIND SHELTERS

You don't get a much more traditional British seaside resort than Blackpool. Situated on England's north-west coast, the town, with its famously long beach, built up its fame when paid holidays for mill workers were first introduced. Over the years, its attractions grew as the idea of the holiday by the sea became ensconced in people's minds. The iconography was particular to the UK – boarding houses, sandwiches with real sand in them, donkey rides, fish and chips, shivering children, deckchairs, and windbreaks set up on the beach and constantly being moved as the wind gusted from different directions.

Blackpool was always brighter and brasher than other destinations, and with the demise of traditional holidaymaking, it reinvented itself as an entertainment venue and home of the political conference. Now it has gone through another transformation, upgrading its funfair and smartening its appearance with, for example, the new two-kilo-metre (1 1/4-mile) South Shore promenade, intended as a venue for artworks. Rebranded as the Great Promenade Show, this offers a number of attractions, one of which is a reinterpretation of that old favourite, the seaside shelter.

In addition to those makeshift windbreaks on the beach, British promenades traditionally offered sheltered seating where one could sit, slightly protected from the wind and rain, in a summer mackintosh looking out over the grey sea and listening to the plaintive cry of seagulls. The Royal Institute of British Architects launched a competition in 2002 to come up with a contemporary interpretation of that shelter, a rotating structure powered by a weather vane that would always have its back to the wind. The competition was won by a little-known architect, Ian McChesney, based in south London, who came up with the idea of a single structure that would act both as vane and shelter. In its final form it looks gratifyingly like a whale's tail, one of the strongest symbols of the sea.

Although the design has since gone through rigorous analysis, including the construction of a full-scale model, it started in a traditionally boffin-like way. McChesney came up with his initial design and tested it with a 30-centimetre (12-inch) high paper model. He stuck a pin through the middle of it, placed it in a dish of water and aimed his desk fan at it. When he found that it wobbled, it was evident that the design needed to be refined. Ironically, by the time that the full-scale model was tested, the aerodynamic design, developed with engineer Atelier One, was just too good. The shelter rotated, but it went too fast for safety, so much of the future effort was dedicated to damping down the movement.

Originally there were to be three shelters, but cost constraints cut them to two. The first one was installed at the start of April 2006, with the second due to be put in place at the end of that sum-mer. The result is certainly handsome and striking. The steel 'whale's tail', 8 metres (26 1/4 feet) high, has a curve in it as if the powerful mammal is about to set off in a new direction, thrashing the water as it does so. At its base is a simple, horseshoe-shaped wooden seat. To reflect the rotation, there is circular patterned paving in different shades and textures of grey.

This is certainly attention-grabbing design, but with an elegance and sophistication of which Blackpool could only have dreamed half a century ago.

Below: From some angles,
the shelter looks like the
tail of a massive marine
creature.

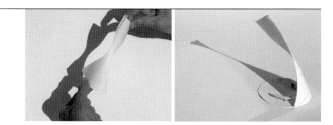

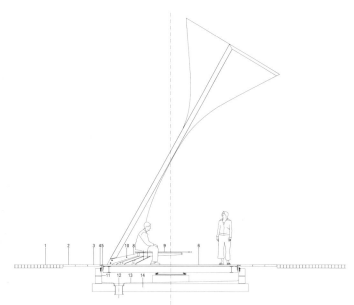

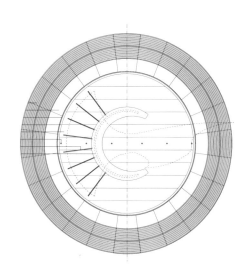

Opposite far left: Section through a shelter and (below) plan showing the horseshoe-shaped seat and contrasting paving.

Left: McChesney made the first models in paper and tested them with a desk fan.

Below: The contemporary shelters contrast with Blackpool's traditional attractions of trams, roller-coaster rides and the iconic Blackpool Tower.

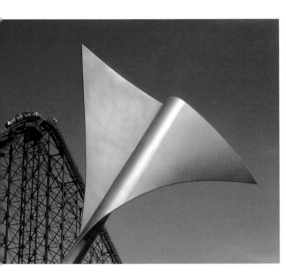

COMMUNITY SPACES

Supermarkets, out-of-town shopping centres, sports arenas and other places of entertainment seem relentlessly to get bigger, driven by economies of scale and the desire to turn a profit. But sometimes, even in the public arena, there is a requirement for somewhere small to serve a restricted or specialist community. And very often these places can be exciting precisely because of the constraints with which they have had to deal.

In retail, the very uniformity that is imposed by large impersonal outlets leads us to appreciate the quirky and individual, which, especially if the objects being shown are not themselves large, can easily be contained in a small area. Archigram founder turned academic Peter Cook has written in the *Architectural Review* (June 2006) about the iconography of food kiosks. Although they seem almost unconsidered, they have an interesting history. The German Modernists of the 1930s, for instance, designed neat little structures to sit at the end of tree-lined boulevards that were exported around the world. 'You can be forgiven, momentarily,' writes Cook, 'for confusing Frankfurt's Holbeinstrasse with Tel Aviv's Ben Yehuda Street, because they share exactly the same model.'

Equally distinctive is the K67 kiosk, a design of polyester-reinforced modules by Slovenian architect Sasha J. Mächtig. Patented in 1967, it was sold not only in the countries of former Yugoslavia but also throughout Eastern Europe, and even in Japan and New Zealand. There is even one in the collection of the Museum of Modern Art in New York.

Architects have also found one-off shop design a good place to develop their skills and reputations. Only in a city with land values as high as those of Tokyo, however, would one be able to justify putting so much care into a tiny plot, as on Klein Dytham's Billboard Building (see page 64).

Miniaturization of shops
does not make the objects
sold any cheaper, but in the
case of hotels, the more one
can reduce the space for
each customer, the less it is
necessary to charge. The
prototype of this approach
is the now famous Japanese
capsule hotel, described
as like 'a plastic coffin'
and usually for men only.
The first, which opened in
Osaka in 1979, was designed
by Kisho Kurokawa.

The concept has migrated
to Europe with, for instance,

budget airline operator
Easy Jet opening EasyHo-
tels in London and Basel,
Switzerland. However, with
the smallest rooms having
a floor area of 6 square metres (64 1/2 square feet),
these are a dilution of the
original concept. So is the
'Yotel' concept, being pio-
neered at London airports,
and offering visitors 10.5-
square-metre (113-square-
foot) capsule rooms with
no external windows. The
attraction, in contrast, of the
Park Hotel in Linz, Austria
(see page 72), is that it takes

this idea right back to basics
and, instead of becoming
sleazy, has some of the joy
and sense of freedom that
one finds in camping – and,
it could be argued, some of
the inconvenience.

All the projects above are
straightforwardly com-
mercial operations, and so
cannot be confused with
the 'public realm' buildings
described in the previous
chapter. For some of the
others discussed here,
however, the lines are less
clearly defined. But they

have earned their place in
this chapter, I believe, either
because they are within
private enterprises, such as
the meditation space and
the chapel, or are intended
for specific groups, whether
they be the bocce players
of Australia or pigeons in
France.

There are reasons for their
small size – reasons either
of finance or of a restricted
community. For example,
providing a place for worship at a housing fair is
laudable, but it is unlikely to

Below: Hawkins\Brown's
small, secure retail units for
Bradbury Street market in
north London were part of
a scheme to regenerate the
area in the late 1990s.

attract many visitors. A large
building would not only
be unnecessarily costly but
would also be daunting.
The one project that is an
exception to the rule is
the SolVin Pretzel by
Gilles Ebersolt (see page
90). Although relatively
small (and with a contained
volume of zero cubic me-
tres!) this has actually been
designed to be as large as
possible. But then, once you
are floating above the tree
tops, it seems reasonable to
discard all the rules of ter-
restrial architecture.

BILLBOARD BUILDING

Tokyo, with its high land values and overcrowding, has a lot of tiny buildings – what local architect Yoshiharu Tsukamoto has dubbed 'pet architecture'. Klein Dytham's Billboard Building sits firmly in this league. Selected by the city's *Ping* magazine as one of the seven lesser-known architectural wonders of Tokyo, it occupies a site that in most cities would be considered unbuildable, or at least not worth bothering with.

It is 11 metres (36 feet) long but only 2.5 metres (8 feet 3 inches) wide – and that is at the wide end. From there it tapers down to only 60 centimetres (23 1/2 inches). Sitting in front of another building, but unrelated to it, it faces a well-used road. Instead of trying to circumvent the near two-dimensional nature of the site, the architect decided to make the most of it, treating it as a billboard. Perhaps best known for its Leaf Chapel for weddings, the practice brings the same sort of decorative playfulness to bear here. The façade is glazed, with a pattern of bamboo stencilled onto it, and the rear wall is painted a bright apple green. During the day, the stencilling helps to provide sunshading, and at night the building glows, introducing a fantasy element of the countryside into the city.

The plan of the two-storey building could not be simpler. Entrance is at the wide end, where there is also a staircase. The prow is occupied on the ground floor by a lavatory and on the first floor by a kitchenette. The structure is of steel, with moulded cement panels where there is not glazing. If the building seems jewel-like, it is therefore appropriate that it is occupied by a jeweller, who calls the shop Acrylic. And somehow, with such a strong architectural conceit, it is not surprising that that jeweller is Masako Ban, wife of the inventive architect Shigeru Ban.

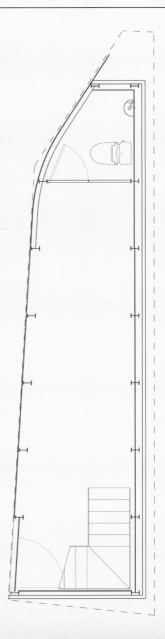

Opposite: Plan of the
narrow building.

Below: The patterning on
the façade gives passers-by
the impression that they are
looking at a grove of trees.

Below left: Only in a city with such high land prices would it be worthwhile building on such a narrow strip of land.

Below centre: At night the building glows through the stencilled patterning.

Below right: During the day, the patterns cast shadows that provide some shade.

S(CH)AUSTALL

Humour runs through this conversion of an old pig shed in Pfalz, Germany, from the playfulness of the architecture to the wit inherent in the name. Now an exhibition space, it is called S(ch)austall in German, punning on Saustall, meaning pigsty, and Schaustall, meaning showroom. It is designed by a Stuttgart-based practice that is, however, intensely serious about its work, and not afraid to impose its ideas on its clients. In a previous project, it succeeded in persuading a hotel operator that creating a 30-room hotel on a site would be entirely inappropriate, and that a 12-room one should be built instead. From this point onward the operator simply left all decisions in the hands of the architect.

With S(ch)austall, FNP Architekten was similarly determined. The client wanted a building on her land to house small exhibitions. 'She had a book about beautiful small buildings,' explained FNP's Martin Naumann. 'She was thinking perhaps of a black box.' But when the architect found the eighteenth-century pig shed he was enchanted. A two-storey structure, originally inhabited not just by pigs but also by their swineherd, it was full of old bins and other junk. But the architect was charmed by both the accretions of age and the position, right next to a country lane. This latter could not be replicated with a new building, as permission would not be given to build so close to the road.

So the architect decided to use this structure for the new building, and convinced the client to accept this decision. Once all the non-original elements had been cleared away, only the shell remained. The next key decision was to insert new interior elements, and to keep them entirely separate structurally. This is the approved way of dealing with historic structures today, and one that the architect decided to embrace, even though in this case the structure was 'only' a ramshackle pig shed.

The interior consists effectively of two timber boxes, one at the front and one at the rear, joined by a short narrow link. Openings in the internal boxes echo the openings in the original structure, although they are slightly narrower, making their presence, in terms of a strip of plywood, visible from outside.

The boxes were prefabricated offsite and craned in, an ambitious exercise since the irregular nature of the existing carapace meant that there were some pinch points to be negotiated. Circulation is changed from the original, with all entrance via a ramp at the back. What was a front door is now just a glazed window, and a low opening for the pigs remains, complete with an external trough and a hinged shutter which is fixed in a half-open position. The whole is topped by a lightweight metal roof, based on the original shallow double pitch but supported entirely on the new structure.

Visitors find themselves following an intriguing route to an interior that is entirely modern but in which the fenestration positions seem charmingly arbitrary until one considers the original usage. Whatever the inherent historic value of this building, the architect has demonstrated that preserving it has allowed the creation of a space that blends new and old in a way that seems entirely appropriate to this rather urban use in a rural environment.

Below left: The new building was designed as two
boxes that were craned into
the old shell.

Below right: Openings in
the interior structure have
been designed so that a
slender border of plywood
is visible from outside.

Below left: Two boxes were inserted, and access provided by a ramp at the back.

Below right: The new roof does not rest on the walls of the original building.

Bottom right: The sleek interior is suited to the housing of small exhibitions.

Opposite: The roughness and wildness of the original building has remained untouched.

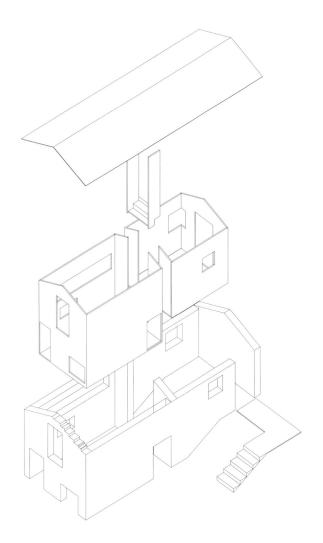

ANDREAS STRAUSS
LINZ, AUSTRIA

DAS PARK HOTEL

All you really need from a hotel room is somewhere to sleep that is secure and reasonably comfortable. How often have we all said that or heard it? Artist Andreas Strauss has taken this idea to the extreme, producing a hotel so minimal that it looks like a student project. The great thing about it, however, is that it actually works. First opening for the Ars Electronica Festival in Linz, Austria, in the summer of 2005, it took 150 bookings – not bad, considering that there were only three rooms available.

As its name suggests, Das Park is set in a park in this genteel Austrian city. The idea is that it need offer no more than a place to sleep. After all, a park has lavatories and showers, and there are plenty of cafés and restaurants around, plus a swimming pool nearby. The 'rooms' consist of concrete drainage pipes (donated by manufacturer C. Bergmann) that each weigh 9 1/2 tonnes. They have been adapted as simply as possible. A small round hole in the top provides light and air. A platform acts as a base for a mattress and sleeping bag, with a small surface with a lamp to one side. The space under the platform is for storage. Most importantly, there is a secure, hinged timber door.

Potential visitors book through a website, and are given a unique code for the electronic lock on the door. When they go, they leave as much money as they consider appropriate. Internally, the surface is finished with a clear varnish, and artist Thomas Latzel Ochoa painted a unique mural on the end wall of each pipe.

The hotel is only intended for use in the summer, and its thermal mass means that it remains cool, even in the hottest weather.

Visitors to Das Park in its first year ranged from local teenagers, using it like a 'love hotel', to visiting Dutch cyclists. The project was only able to get off the ground because of arts funding, but Strauss is keen to keep the idea going – and extend it. He is already in talks with an organization in Slovenia, and is also looking at the possibility of using solar power to provide electricity for the locks, if a location is chosen that cannot easily be cabled.

And if it doesn't prove a success? Well, says Strauss, you simply remove the 20 screws that hold the door, end panel and interior platform in place, and the hotel reverts to a series of drainage pipes, ready to be placed in the ground and do the job for which they were originally intended.

Below left: A hinged, lock-
able door provides access to
each of the 'hotel' rooms.

Below right: Each pipe
contains one room in a
parkland setting.

Bottom right: Murals by
Thomas Latzel Ochoa en-
liven the interior, which has
been designed simply but
ergonomically.

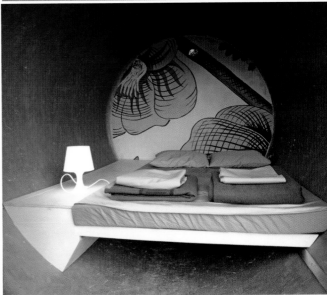

PATJARR VISITOR CENTRE

Australia may be one of the most affluent countries in the world but its harsh internal geography means that it still has vast scarcely populated spaces, remote from the centres of population. It is also still dealing with the legacy of its ill-treatment of aboriginal people and is attempting to make amends by showing respect to them.

One aboriginal group is the Patjarr community, now numbering around 50, including artists of international renown. They are based in the Gibson Desert in Western Australia, about 600 kilometres (370 miles) west of Uluru, but they have not always been there. During the 1960s, when their home area was used for missile testing, they were relocated to Warburton, 240 kilometres (150 miles) to the southeast, and only came back in the 1980s. Despite their remoteness there is considerable interest in their work and there was a desire to create a centre where it could be shown and sold – a facility both for the community and for tourists.

Given the difficulty of access, the most obvious location was beside the airstrip – what some have described as a 'fly-in fly-out' visitor centre. Money was found in the form of $Aus 82,000 from the regional lottery, and the project was designed by students at the University of South Australia under the direction of lecturers David Morris and Nick Opie.

There were a number of key considerations for the building. The budget was tight, particularly given the remoteness of the site. It had to be prefabricated and transportable to the site, and capable of being erected in a relatively short period by unskilled (i.e. student) labour. And it had to be able to cope with the climatic conditions.

The two final-year students who did the design, Oli Scholz and Niko Young, came up with a lightweight steel portal frame that uses cold-rolled steel stud framing for the walls and timber sub-framing for the ceilings. Steel is a durable material,

appropriate for the desert where there is a need to resist termites.

Cladding is with corrugated steel sheet, polycarbonate glazing and jarrah hardwood slatting – again tough materials for a building that will receive little maintenance. The low-pitched roofs have large overhangs to provide solar shading and, with the glazing at clerestory level just below these roofs, there should be little solar gain.

The building has a concrete floor to provide some thermal mass, and there is also insulation in the walls and ceiling to cope with the wide range of temperatures in the desert. This is also a building that has to close up tightly so that it can be dustproof in the case of dust storms.

The building was fabricated in the university's workshops in Adelaide and then had to travel more than 2,500 kilometres (1,550 miles) to the site, including more than 600 kilometres (370 miles) on gravel roads. Forty students from

the University of South Australia and the University of New South Wales (in Sydney) erected it over a three-week period. Tragically, Nick Opie died of a stroke one week into the construction project, which he was supervising, but the students elected to carry on with the work.

Now open, the building is a relatively modest one, except for its location – which must inspire everybody flying in to wonder how exactly it got there.

Below: The building had to be relatively simple to construct, with low maintenance requirements.

Right: The 'fly-in fly-out' centre is located next to an airstrip.

Below left: Designed to be light and airy, the building can shut down tightly when threatened with dust storms.

Below right: Internationally renowned aboriginal artists display their work at the visitor centre.

Below: The building is
in a remote part of the
Gibson Desert.

BOCCE PAVILION

Bocce is an Italian ball game, very similar to the French boules or pétanque, and related to the English bowls. Like them, it involves rolling a ball along the ground to get it as close as possible to a target ball. Although requiring skill, it does not demand enormous levels of physical fitness and so is popular among older people. This makes it a valuable piece of social glue for ageing emigrant communities, and this is exactly the situation in Melbourne.

The Montemurro Bocce Club, named after the village in Basilicata, southern Italy, from which all the original members had emigrated after World War II, was the first such club in Australia. It established itself first in Princes Park and then moved to the North Carlton Railway Station Neighbourhood House. This was a conversion of a nineteenth-century brick-built railway station and platform, about 7 kilometres (4 1/4 miles) from the city centre, into community facilities. A modest lavatory block was built next to it.

However, the bocce players outgrew this space, so local architect Antonio Di Mase, of Di Mase Architects, designed a new pavilion for them, at one end of the station building. This would give them a room of their own, in which they could put material on display, store their paraphernalia, and play cards when it rained. Despite the modesty of the project, it had a difficult gestation, having to battle both for funding and for permission to change and extend the end of the building.

In contrast to the very solid, brick-built station, the pavilion has a more temporary appearance. It is steel-framed and clad in corrugated metal. There is an entrance at one side, and the front elevation has a shaded veranda overlooking the four bocce 'rinks'. Timber-framed glazed doors open onto it, imparting a domestic feel. Shade comes from an extension of the main curved roof, which gives a certain grandeur internally to an essentially modest building while still being low enough to allow views beyond of the station building and its chimneys. Inside, the curved ceiling is painted a bright sky blue.

The pavilion adds a sense of presence to the bocce rinks, while also making watching and waiting a more pleasurable experience. It provides a place of retreat from sun, from rain and from summer heat. One might think that the ageing emigrant population would slowly die out and the need for the pavilion wither away. But there is an understated allure to these games and the traditional sociability that goes with them that seems to ensure their survival. It is always charming to see a tentative forty-something joining their elders, glad to be welcomed into the circle while also regretfully waving goodbye to their youth.

Which may be no bad analogy for this little pavilion, sitting against its more solid forebear and yet rapidly establishing its importance, its self-possession and its right to be there.

Below: Plan of the pavilion and adjoining building.
1: Entry;
2: Terrace;
3: Bocce pavilion;
4: Garden;

5: Ramp;
6: Female WC;
7: Store;
8: Male WC;
9: Neighbourhood house;
10: Veranda

Bottom left: The shaded terrace overlooks the bocce rinks.

Bottom right: The curved roof gives a certain grandeur to this little building, which serves as a hub of sociability.

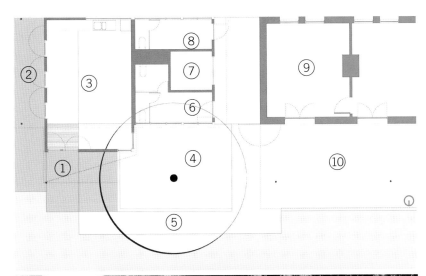

VESA OIVA ARKKITEHTI
OULU, FINLAND

LILJA MEDITATIVE CHAPEL

Designing a building for a religious purpose is one of the most demanding tasks of architecture today, and the requirement that it should be an ecumenical space with no obvious Christian symbolism can make it more difficult. It is a challenge to which Finnish student Vesa Oiva rose magnificently, with a building that uses modest materials to create a numinous space.

Oiva's was the winning entry in a competition organized by timber company UPM-Kymmene with the Wood Studio at the University of Oulu to create a meditative space that could find its first use at the Oulu Housing Fair. These fairs tend to be hectic, so the idea of a place for relaxation was attractive. Oiva came up with the concept of a three-pronged building that was triangular in section, reminiscent of the nave of a church. Constructed in plywood and glulam (glued laminated timber), it has only one decorative element. That is a tree, cut out of birch plywood, and sandwiched between two layers of glass, clear on the outside and opaque on the inside. The tree, which is represented only by its complex interweaving branches, throws attractive shadows into the interior. The chapel itself, in the widest, tallest and shortest arm of the structure, has an interior finish entirely of pale timber, with simple box benches as the only furniture.

With the sun in the right direction, light falls through the tree to cast shadows on the ground, reminiscent of the forest that plays such a large part in the Finns' sense of their own identity, even today. Gently animistic nature worship replaces any more overt religious symbolism, in a space that certainly provides a refuge from the hurly-burly outside.

From the exterior, the chapel is intriguing, opening up like the flap of a tent to lure visitors in. The outside is clad with SP plywood panels, a kind of birch or combination plywood that has a weatherproof painting base and sealed edges. In this case, the plywood has been painted white.

Another condition of the design was that it should be possible to erect and disassemble the structure relatively easily, so that after the fair it could be taken down, stored and then reassembled. The intention is that it should find a permanent home.

In the meantime, Oiva has formed a practice with another fellow student, Selina Anttinen. Just as the building has more impact than its relatively small size might suggest, so winning the competition has provided a good start to a career.

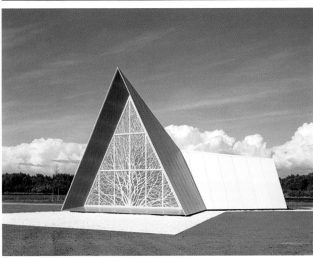

Top left: The chapel itself has a decorative window in the form of a tree.

Centre left: Triangular entrances entice visitors in.

Bottom left: The exterior is of white-painted plywood.

Below: Section and plan of the chapel building.

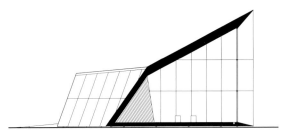

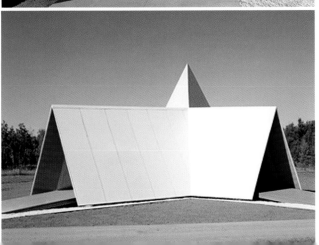

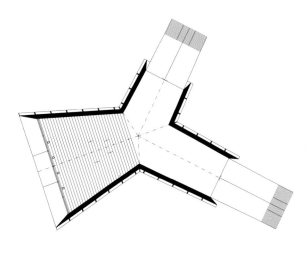

Opposite: The silhouette
of a tree, set between two
layers of glass, provides the
only decorative element in
the chapel.

Below: Pale timber and
simple seating combine
with the triangular forms
to provide a peaceful
atmosphere.

MEDITATION DOME

Garden festivals are big business, showcasing much more than just plants. In the Netherlands, the Floriade, which is held once every ten years, has also become a showcase for imaginative architecture. At Haarlemmermeer, the Catholic and Protestant churches jointly funded a 'silence centre' or 'meditation dome'.

Jord den Hollander drew on a wide variety of sources for inspiration. The form of his dome echoes Rome's Pantheon, a dome with an oculus at the centre that allows the light to change with time and the varying moods of the sky. Unlike the Pantheon, however, his dome has a floor area of only 80 square metres (860 square feet), and rather than being of solid concrete and brick is lightly steel-framed. Cleverly, he spiralled a translucent hose over its surface, so that those inside were aware of both the sight and sound of running water. As well as being soothing, the sound provided aural insulation from what was going on outside.

The structure consists of 16 light square-section ribs in a 9-metre (29 1/2-foot) radius, running from the ground up to the edge of the oculus. At three levels they are joined together by circular steel tubes. The topmost of these, with a diameter of 1 metre (3 feet 3 inches), support the hardened glass of the oculus. Unlike the Pantheon, this oculus is not open to the elements – a reflection of the less clement climate in the Netherlands than in Rome.

Resistance to lateral wind forces and to torsion comes from a secondary rigging of slender steel wires running diagonally along the external surface to form an open diamond-shaped mesh. The steel-reinforced plastic tube that carries the water is then wound around the framework to create the 'cladding' and fixed to it with plastic tie wraps. In total, 2,500 metres (8,202 feet) of tube is needed, made up from 50 pieces each 50 metres (164 feet) long. They were joined on site and then installed with the help of a special truck that circled the structure again and again, resulting no doubt in a somewhat dizzy driver.

Like all such projects, the resulting building, although much appreciated by visitors to the Floriade, was left homeless when the festival came to an end. Various new uses within the Netherlands were suggested but came to nothing. It has now been sold to a welfare group in France, which plans to use it as a Meditation Dome at a health centre for patients with HIV.

Below left: At the top of the structure is an oculus reminiscent of the Pantheon in Rome.

Below right: A haven of tranquillity at the Floriade.

Bottom: After the main structure and secondary rigging were in place, a hose was coiled around the structure.

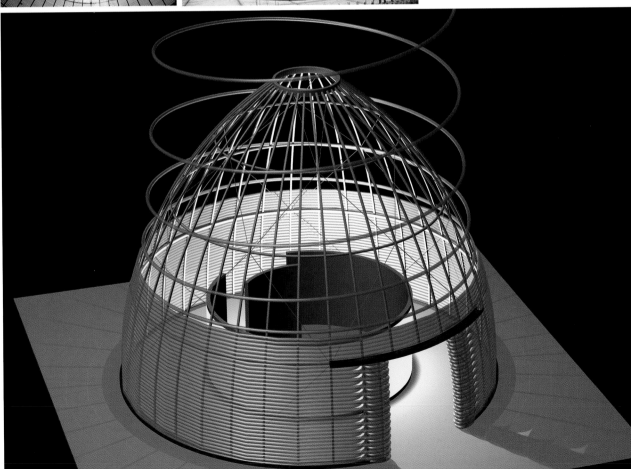

CAPSULE PIGEON LOFT

We have an ambiguous relationship with pigeons. On the one hand they are increasingly seen as pests in towns; on the other hand, many bird lovers cherish them and there is an illustrious working-class tradition of pigeon fancying that grew out of the earlier utilitarian role of pigeons as carriers of messages (and sources of cheap protein). In the age of email and instant messaging, this role is likely to disappear without some outside help.

Surprisingly, the two problems of pest control and dying traditions are not mutually exclusive. The Pigeon Control Advisory Service (PiCAS), an independent, international and non profit-making body, advocates a stick and carrot approach to the menace of birds in towns. First, create a haven where birds can roost and be fed, and then impose fines on the feeding of birds elsewhere in the town.

In cities where pigeons are a real menace, such as Melbourne, Australia, this strategy is accompanied by replacing real eggs in the pigeon loft with dummy ones, to reduce numbers further. But this is not the strategy in Caudry in the flat Nord-Pas de Calais region of France. Worried about their hobby dying out, an association of pigeon fanciers obtained money from an arts fund to pay for the commissioning and construction of a futuristic pigeon loft in the Parc de Loisirs.

The idea was that an eye-catching design would first grab the attention of those previously uninterested in the sport, then fire some of them up with a desire to know more, and eventually breed a new generation of aficionados. With that as an aim, the appointment of Paris-based rising superstar of design Matali Crasset was inspired.

Crasset, a designer who at one stage worked with Philippe Starck and now operates on her own account, has a striking, slightly faux naif approach to design, epitomized by her marketing logo which is based on her own face with its trade-mark Joan of Arc haircut. Most of her work has been in the design of relatively small products, although she has also styled a cutting-edge hotel in Nice.

The result in Caudry is a bright, intriguing object that certainly cannot be ignored, a 'capsule' of bright orange resin, 6 metres (19 feet 7 inches) high and 5 metres (16 feet 4 inches) in diameter, elevated from the ground on a metal post. Shiny metal rods also protrude through the openings, and a jaunty red cube hangs from one of them. Internally a tree trunk complete with branches has been installed to provide roosting points for the pigeons, and there are also nesting boxes around the walls.

Crasset may seem slick and fashionable, but she takes her design seriously and in this case researched the habits of pigeons, so that they should be content with their new home. Although traditionalist pigeon fanciers may look askance at her design, it is hard to ignore and should fulfil its brief of raising awareness. If it leads to a resurgence of enthusiasm for pigeon racing, then one day the Crasset capsule may be seen as the traditional design for a flourishing sport.

Below: The red cube
hanging from one of
the protruding metal
'branches' acts like a
marker for the project.

Below: Sitting on a slight
eminence overlooking the
town of Caudry, the pigeon
loft has a deliberately for-
ward-looking design.

Below left: Crasset, an avant-garde designer but also a farmer's daughter, made a careful study of the habits of pigeons before starting her design.

Bottom left: Part of the purpose of the building is to educate the next generation about the importance and habits of pigeons.

Below right: The capsule is built up (from bottom) a metal 'tree', a timber structure and then a resin shell.

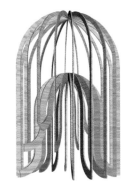

SOLVINPRETZEL

Paris-based Gilles Ebersolt enjoys creating inflatables and floating objects, some merely for fun, some for extreme sports and a whole series of them for scientists who are interested in investigating the forest canopy.

One of the fascinating things about forests is that their ecology is striated – a different ecosystem exists at the top of the canopy compared to that on the ground. But for those who want to study this area, the problem is how to get there. It is an issue that Ebersolt has addressed over the years, working with a number of scientists who were interested in examining the canopy. Although this can be done from a hot-air balloon, it is a noisy and restrictive way of working. It is much better to create a platform that will sit on top of the trees while the study goes on.

The most important aspect of such an object is that it must be light enough just to perch on the canopy, and not tip over or be carried down. Ebersolt developed a series of 'tree-top rafts'

using inflatable structures between which he stretched strong but lightweight fabric. The latest iteration is what he calls the SolVin Pretzel. SolVin is the company that makes the PVC resins used in the inflatable structure of the raft, and pretzel is simply the ubiquitous salted snack. Take a look at the shape, and it soon becomes clear where the name comes from.

This was not some mere sculptural conceit. The important thing with these 'rafts', in addition to lightness, is that they should be as stable as possible. Ebersolt discovered that they would operate best if there were no element of structure at the centre, which could cause a hinge to form and allow it to fold in on itself.

He experimented with a number of shapes, including the triangle, the oval and the hexagon (the last of these was the form of his third-generation raft), before lighting on the pretzel for this, the fourth generation. Because you can draw

the shape without taking the pencil off the paper, it is possible to construct it as one continuous inflatable structure. This is what has been done, with the pretzel in PVC, and a polypropylene mesh platform set within it.

The result is spectacular. Weighing only 500 kilos (1,100 pounds), the raft has a surface area of 400 square metres (4,305 square feet). It is lifted into place by a helicopter or an airship, and can support four

people. In one case, researchers even camped on it overnight in a tent.

Few will see the full glory of the construction in situ since, even if they were passing through that particular section of remote rainforest, it would be obscured by the trees overhead. But before it went off to Central America to start serious work, Ebersolt erected it in Paris at Saint-Cloud, as part of an exhibition on the art of the garden. Not surprisingly, it was a crowd puller.

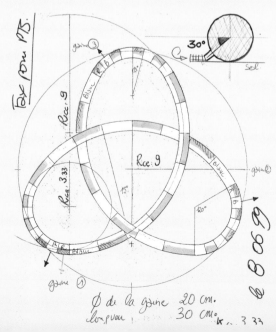

Opposite: Ebersolt's initial drawing of the 'pretzel'.

Below left top: The 'pretzel' is designed to sit on the forest canopy.

Below left centre: The raft was so stable that one night four people were able to camp on it in a tent.

Below left bottom: Polypropylene mesh is fixed to the inflatable PVC tubes of the structure.

Below right: The raft can be installed by an inflatable craft.

ON THE MOVE

Nomadism arguably precedes architecture, and certainly the architecture of fixed communities that we see today and which forms our architectural heritage. Both pure nomads, hunters who moved from place to place, and pastoral nomads, who were seeking seasonal pasture for their animals, lived in temporary shelters. Some nomadic peoples still live similarly today: the Tuareg in the Niger with their structures woven from locally available plant materials, the Mongolians with their *gers* or yurts, wooden frameworks covered in felt, or the Siberian people with their tepee-like *ursas*, or poles with caribou hides laid over them.

But apart from a few hippy-like folk embracing the idea of the yurt, the dwellings of these fairly marginalized people have had little influence on mainstream architecture.

Although the tent is usually either a basic structure in which to rough it, or a high-tech solution for people in extreme environments, it

has another and darker use. One of the sights following any disaster, natural or man-made, is the sea of tents that springs up to house refugees. In many environments they do not provide adequate shelter, so inventive minds have turned to creating better alternatives while still keeping the advantages of low cost and speed of delivery and erection.

There are also more fanciful solutions, such as Japanese designer Takehiko Sanada's Prefab Coat, which has been widely exhibited in Canada. Sanada, who worked for seven years for that master of fabrics, Issey Miyake, has designed a garment in recycled polyester which, when unzipped, can be supported on poles and used as a shelter. Romantically, two people can zip their coats together to form a tent for two. And larger numbers can also create an appropriately larger dwelling. Sanada has written, 'This work represents how a diverse group of people from different regions can open their hearts to cover and embrace a new world.'

This page: Prefab Coat by Takehiko Sanada. Re-cycled polyester garments can be zipped together to form a shelter for one or several people.

Below left: The Basecamp, a new offering from Airstream, can be towed behind a vehicle and is described as a 'multi-purpose tent-trailer'.

Below right: Basecamp interiors are sleek and modern.

Much more in tune with most people's notion of mobility is the idea of a dwelling on wheels. Traditionalists may plump for the horse-drawn Romany vardo or caravan; others prefer the internal combustion engine.

Mobility has a particular attraction for large numbers of people in the United States, harking back to the covered wagons of the pioneers crossing the continent and also to an idealized vision of the footloose hobo. Travel writer Richard Grant, in his book *Ghost Riders: Travels with American Nomads*, describes both the history of American nomadism and its appeal today.

Some of these people on the move are 'snowbirds', fleeing the cold winters of the north and east for the warmer temperatures of the south. And although travellers, they are not necessarily loners, meeting for example in huge numbers in Quartzsite, Arizona every January and February.

These modern-day travellers' home of choice is the RV (recreational vehicle), which tends to be functional and even comfortable, but ugly. There are, however, exceptions, the best known of which is the sleek aluminium Airstream trailer that has become a design classic. A towed vehicle rather than an all-in-one, it is now available in alternative formats,

such as a mobile office and also the Basecamp, another elegant solution which the company describes as 'a lightweight multi-purpose tent-trailer'.

Some of the projects in this chapter subvert the aesthetics of the RV, while others throw down a challenge to our perceptions of how we want to live. For example, Andrea Zittel's A-Z Wagon Stations, (see page 110) are a deliberate attempt to slip between the cracks of consumerist society, while architect Jay Shafer, whose work is superficially so much more conformist, is demonstrating with the XS House just how much it is possible to live without (see page 122).

Whether they are concerned with creating an exhibition space from washing machines, breaking down the barriers between inside and outside in the middle of woodland, or turning the workaday shipping container into a plush marketing suite, all the projects here make us think again about some of our preconceived ideas – whether those ideas are to do with homes or leisure or even our conventional expectations of a theatre.

FOREST REFUGE

Barcelona-based ex.studio is a practice whose members are as interested in art and ideas as they are in designing buildings. Although they have created actual objects – ranging from some interventions in apartments to lights and other accessories – the two Mexican architects who founded the practice, Iván Juárez and Patricia Meneses, devote as much attention to theoretical reinterpretations of the way that people relate to their environment as they do to straightforward architectural commissions.

One of these strands of interest concerns ideas of containment and observation. In a conventional building we have rigid barriers between the interior, which we control, and the outside, which is alien. Exchange between the two is only mediated through the windows, which bring in air or rain or smells or flies or even intruders. Shut the windows, block up the chimney, close the ventilation ducts and you will be sealed off from everything except, probably, sound. Although Proust,

in his cork-lined bedroom, managed even that.

Once we step outside we experience the opposite extreme. Then we are at the mercy of the external world, protected by nothing more than our skins and clothes. And if we are going to spend any time in nature, we are going to have to create a new protective container – a cabin, a tent or a vehicle – that may be more permeable and less comfortable than our home, but still creates a definite barrier. What interests Juárez and Meneses is the possibility of creating an enclosure that is not fixed, that provides some protection from the environment while at the same time responding to it. This also makes it far less intrusive. As with the birdwatcher in his hide who is unnoticed by the creatures around him, Forest Refuge allows its inhabitants to be participants in the larger scene – but unlike the birdwatcher they are not restricted just to the sensations of sight and sound but also have the sensations of touch and movement.

Forest Refuge is a kind of bubble to contain people. Supported by a strong but flexible wire frame, it is covered by an elastic textile skin that will be distorted by its surroundings – the ground on which it sits, the bodies of its inhabitants, the trees against which it leans. For complete integration with the surroundings, it can be covered with leaves and made virtually invisible. By contrast, putting a light inside it at night creates a kind of eerily glowing object. If it is left in situ for a while, one can easily imagine forest life carrying on regardless of this alien object, allowing its inhabitants excellent possibilities for observation.

The practice obviously relishes the idea of this type of semi-permeable enclosure. Another project, Dream House, was a kind of giant teardrop suspended from a tree, large enough for one person to inhabit and, again, beautifully lit at night. The architects describe it as 'an interior place for self-reflection', although whether those reflections take the

form of dreams or nightmares probably depends on how claustrophobic you are.

Below: When lit from inside
the refuge has a somewhat
eerie presence.

Bottom: The refuge's wire
structure is flexible enough
to adjust to the form of its
surroundings.

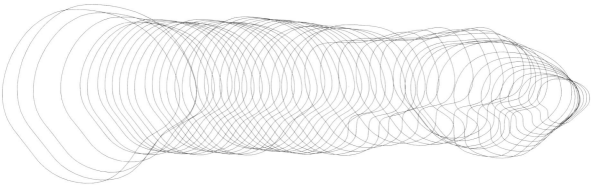

TOM EBDON, LEE HALLIGAN, PETER GROVE
MOJAVE DESERT, CALIFORNIA, USA

THERMALWING

Three young architects from the UK, Tom Ebdon, Lee Halligan and Peter Grove, won a competition in 2005 to design a 'green tent' for use in California's Mojave Desert, just north of Joshua Tree National Park. The organizer, Ecoshack, which is based there, said that it was looking for 'innovative ideas inspired by southern California's green lifestyle'. It is an organization that describes its goal as 'to bring a little more fringe mentality to mainstream culture and commerce.' The solution that the trio came up with was certainly innovative, a recognition that in that climate one does not need enclosure but a method of regulating the temperature, of keeping cool during the day and warm at night.

The solution is called Thermalwing, and it looks more like a hang-glider than anything else. The large wing, with a shiny surface covering most of it, stands on a pivoting leg. During the day it provides shelter from the heat and the sun. Then at night it is lowered to reflect heat and light onto the people sleeping beneath it.

The trio was invited, in October 2005, to build and sleep under their creation in the desert, over a ten-day period. They built three of them, aligning each to have views of a different mountain, and slept underneath them. The cost per unit was just a fraction under £1,000 (about $1,800).

In the environment of Ecoshack, sleeping outside with no privacy or protection is both acceptable and a challenge. It is a solution that is unlikely to win many fans in other places, but as an exercise in practical architecture and creative thinking, it was certainly worthwhile.

Opposite: The three Thermalwings were positioned to have views of different mountains.

Below left: Has a hang-glider landed in the desert?

Bottom left: Lifted in the day to provide shade, at night the wide part of the Thermalwing can be lowered to reflect body heat back onto people sleeping beneath it.

Below right: This is a very basic notion of shelter that does not disrupt connections with the surrounding land.

CONCRETE CANVAS SHELTER

Housing of refugees and other homeless people is a popular project amongst students, but too often the ideas are far too elaborate – students keen to use their imagination do not want to ground it with harsh realities. A project initiated when its developers were studying at London's Royal College of Art, however, is deeply imbued with practicality and close to coming into production. Called Concrete Canvas, it proposed a permanent alternative to the tent, which would be almost as easy and fast to erect but would last for up to ten years. The first objection is, of course, that it does not have a tent's mobility, but in fact too many people end up using a tent as a semi-permanent homes, even though it has a maximum life of only about two years. The important thing is the initial ease of deployment, not the subsequent mobility.

Interestingly, neither of the two men behind Concrete Canvas Technology is an architect. Peter Brewin and Will Crawford both studied industrial design engineering at the Royal College of Art in London, following first degrees in, respectively, engineering and mechanical engineering. Both have taken part in expeditions to remote places, and have experience with the army and the Ministry of Defence in Britain. Perhaps as a result, they have concentrated on function rather than appearance.

Concrete Canvas is the third project on which the two have worked together, and it has won them several prestigious prizes. They are in the process of seeking funding that will allow them to take it into full-scale production. The product consists of a cement-impregnated fabric that is bonded to an inflatable plastic liner. Weighing 230 kilos (506 pounds) dry, it is delivered folded in a sealed plastic sack, which eight people can lift. It is light enough to be transported in a pick-up truck or a light aircraft.

Once in position, the sack is filled with reasonably clean water – i.e. anything except sewage or seawater. The amount of water needed is 120 litres (26 1/2 gallons), (the United Nations daily ration for 12 people) and is controlled by the volume of the sack. This is important since it removes the possibility for error.

After 15 minutes, the concrete will have hydrated, and the sack is then cut along its seams, and forms part of the groundsheet. This should be done at dusk, to avoid over-drying the cement. Next a chemical pack is activated which releases a controlled volume of gas into the plastic inner liner and inflates the structure into its final form, rather like a Nissen hut. The inflation is key since it supports the concrete structure during curing, allowing a very thin layer of concrete to be used. Nevertheless, because of the shape, the finished structure will be very strong in compression and also earthquake-resistant. After 12 hours, when the concrete has cured, the inner liner can be deflated and holes cut in it where it was left bare to form doors.

Because of the compressive strength, other materials can be piled on top of the structure – earth, sandbags or snow. This will improve the thermal performance and can also provide protection against bombardment. The standard form of Concrete Canvas provides a surface area internally of 16 square metres (172 square feet), but it can be scaled up to provide up to 30 square metres (322 square feet), for functions such as storage of food or equipment.

The inventors also foresee other applications, such as agricultural storage or accommodation. But, in an emergency situation, there will be some limit to the period of usefulness.

Despite the inherent strength of the structure, its thin wall makes it easy to demolish with hand tools – and there is not even much material to dispose of. Even at demolition stage, the developers show the attention to detail that makes their proposal seem so attractive and viable.

Below: The two engineers have designed a process that is both simple and almost foolproof.

Bottom left: A completed prototype, with door.

Bottom right: A building delivered in a bag rapidly becomes a concrete structure, supported by an inflatable inner liner while it cures.

Delivery

Hydration

Inflation

Setting

DESERT SEAL

Tents have advantages but also limitations. They are lightweight and provide some shelter from the elements, although this is mostly just keeping the rain out. But in an arid environment, they scarcely moderate the temperature at all.

This is the issue that London- and Munich-based Architecture and Vision has addressed with its Desert Seal prototype. Intended for some of the harshest environments – it can be transported by camel and emulates the behaviour of certain reptiles – it uses some advanced technology. This is a reflection of the background of the founders of the practice – Arturo Vittori has worked as an architect at Airbus in Toulouse and Andreas Vogler researched space architecture with NASA in Houston. Having looked imaginatively at designing for the difficult environments in space, they have then translated their ideas to some of the least forgiving places on earth.

Deserts are difficult environments because they are intensely hot in the day and equally cold at night. The most extreme temperatures are experienced close to the ground – move up just 1 metre (3 feet 3 inches) or so and they become more moderate. Desert Seal exploits this gradient in its design.

It is a tent, but very different from the standard shape. It is shaped like a boomerang (the designers describe it as 'anticlastic', which is defined as 'having transverse and opposite curvatures of surface'), so that it lies along the ground and then curves up at one end to be 2.1 metres (6 feet 9 inches) tall. At the top is a fan that brings in cool air during the day and warm air at night. This has the added advantage of making it possible to enter the tent in a standing position. An advanced solar-power unit runs the fan during the day, and replenishes a battery that runs it at night.

The structure consists of two bright yellow 'air beams' of polyurethane-coated polyethylene that are inflated to provide support. The outer skin is of a high-technology lightweight silver fabric that will reflect external heat during the day, and help to retain heat inside at night.

The lightweight nature of the materials allows the tent to be folded into a small space, and could mean the difference not just between comfort and discomfort but, in the extreme, between life and death.

Below: Alongside 'horses designed by committee' (as camels are sometimes known), the form of the tents seems less outlandish.

Below centre: The tents are designed for ease of transport and erection.

Bottom: The unconventional form and the fan take maximum advantage of the temperature gradients above the ground.

Transport

Roll-out and fixing

Development

Operation

Below: One person can stretch out comfortably in the tent.

Bottom: The tent packs up small, and can be inflated with a foot pump.

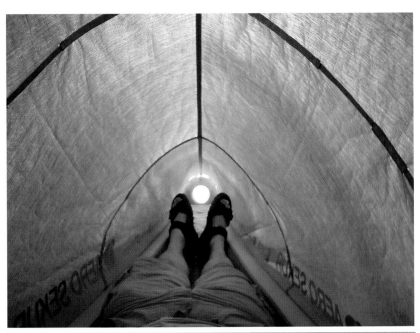

CARDBOARD HOUSE

Cardboard is not an obvious building material, but its potential for construction has been realized recently by several architects, including the Japanese Shigeru Ban with his houses made from cardboard tubes, and Cottrell & Vermeulen Architecture in the UK, which designed an award-winning school largely constructed from cardboard.

One of the latest practices to be attracted to the idea is the Australian firm Stutchbury and Pape, which designed a prototype cardboard house for the House of the Future exhibition staged in Sydney Olympic Park in 2005. It worked with another architect, who has passionate environmental briefs and had previously worked with a student of his at Sydney University to develop a bay of a house made from paper and cardboard. In this latest project, the architects wanted not just to develop a house that could be afforded by people for whom conventional housing was unaffordable, but also to look at simplified ways of living and to design something that had virtually no environmental impact.

Their solution is an A-framed house, built of cardboard members interlocked together for structural strength, in a similar way to the interlocking of the elements inside a wine box. The aim was that the house should be as easy to assemble as flat-pack furniture – or perhaps that should read 'easier to assemble than …', given how common it is to have problems with the furniture.

Although the intention is that the design should be flexible enough to allow variations – for instance service pods for a kitchen and bathroom can be either inside or out on the veranda – the prototype evidently has to take one form. For this the architects have settled on five bays, two for a living area, one for a bathroom and two for a kitchen, with a sleeping platform on the mezzanine above. The fixings are nylon wing nuts, hand-tightened polyester stays and Velcro, and the architects calculate that it should take two people only six hours to erect the structure.

To protect the house from rain, there is a waterproof overlayer, a sheet of hdpe (high-density polyethylene) that acts like a flysheet on a tent, helping to hold the house down as well as keeping out the rain. The same material is used for rainwater-storage bladders under the floor, and also for the construction of the bathroom and kitchen pods. The weight of the bladders also helps to hold down the structure.

Everything has been designed to be as environmentally friendly as possible. The cardboard is made from material that is 90 per cent recycled, there is a composting lavatory, rainwater harvesting and low-voltage lighting that can be powered by a solar panel.

With assembly (and disassembly) so simple, this counts as a movable, temporary dwelling. It weighs only about 2,000 kilos (4,400 pounds) and can easily be delivered on a truck flatbed. Although the look is a mile away from conventional housing, the articulation of the structure internally provides an attractive appearance – and even potential shelving!

The architects believe that, at a cost of only about Aus $35,000, this could prove an appealing option for people who would otherwise be priced out of the housing market.

The interlocking elements
give strength to what is
inherently quite a flimsy
material.

Below left: Visitors to the Future exhibition in Sydney were intrigued.

Below right: The waterproof covering acts like a flysheet on a tent.

Bottom left: A pivoting section of side wall doubles as an entrance and a shade canopy.

Bottom right. Top lighting and a mezzanine sleeping area allow maximum use to be made of the space.

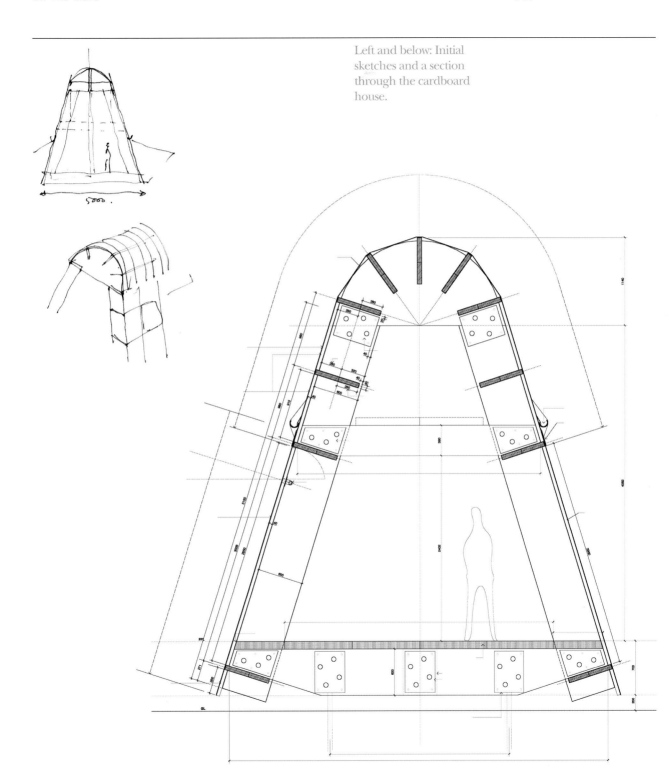

Left and below: Initial
sketches and a section
through the cardboard
house.

ANDREA ZITTEL
CALIFORNIA, USA

A-Z WAGON STATIONS

Andrea Zittel is an artist whose work addresses all aspects of her life. Having started in New York, where she designed clothing and furniture and interior elements to define her way of living, she moved back to her native California, to Joshua Tree in the California desert. There her experiments continued, with one of the latest being Wagon Stations, a deliberate play on the idea of the station wagon.

Zittel makes reference not only to this twentieth-century model but also to an earlier idea, the wagon trains that crossed America. Her wagons, however, are moved neither by horses nor by the internal combustion engine. Because they are light and can be broken down into five sections, the idea is that individuals can carry them from one spot to another.

At present, however, a number of them have found a place on her land. Built in aluminium, and shaped like oversized bread bins on legs, they are being occupied by Zittel's friends, many of whom have set about customizing them. For example, fellow artist Hal McFeely has made his deliberately rough and ready, by using the discarded wood and broken-down crates that are freely available from the nearby Twenty Nine Palms Air Ground Combat Center.

This is a far cry from the much slicker versions that Zittel exhibited at the Milwaukee Art Museum in 2003 where identical units, lined up side by side, had a futuristic and somewhat forbidding look. But this is typical of Zittel's approach, which she draws together under the heading A-Z Living at her base, A-Z West. Zittel herself describes it in the following way: 'The A-Z Wagon Station reflects the qualities that we believe create independence for the owner and user: compactness, adaptability and transportability. 'The original pioneering spirit of the "frontier" considered autonomy and self-sufficiency as prerequisites of personal freedom. Here at A-Z West we are continuing to investigate how such perceptions of freedom have been re-adapted for contemporary living. We believe that, presently, personal liberation is more often achieved through individual attempts to "slip between the cracks". Instead of building big ranches and permanent homesteads, today's independence seekers prefer small portable structures, which evade the regulatory control of bureaucratic restrictions such as building and safety codes.'

When closed up, the Wagon
Stations have an enigmatic
appearance in the uncom-
promising desert landscape
of California.

Below left: Artist Hal McFeely customized his wagon with discarded crates.

Below right: Back to back wagons on public exhibition. Customized by Andrea Zittel and David Dodge.

Bottom: Internally, the wagons can be made into whatever type of refuge the user desires. Customized by Jennifer Nocon

Left: Zittel believes that the wagons, which are light enough to be transported by hand, can help recreate a pioneering spirit. This example was customized by Veronica Fernandez and Peter Blackburn.

SUMMER CONTAINER

What does a Los Angeles-based real-estate company have to do with a Finnish architectural academic? Unlikely as the pairing may seem, the answer is that the real-estate company, Mossler & Doe, is representing the movable holiday home that the academic, architect Markku Hedman (of MH Cooperative), has developed. Think again and it doesn't seem quite so daft, since this is one of the areas where the usually very dissimilar cultures of Californian hedonism and northern European extremes coincide.

The Finnish seem to have a hard-wired relationship with their forests. A huge proportion of the population actually owns a patch of woodland, and these forests, which cover the majority of the landmass, are the natural sites for recreation. They are for the Finns a source of respite from the long winters, a place to escape to on the long summer days and get back in touch with the soil that has been hidden for so much of the year. And what better way for an inhabitant of this design-conscious nation to take themselves into the woods than in an elegant transportable home?

For Americans, it is the movement rather than the woodland that is atavistic. Markku Hedman's concept is for a neat and simple dwelling that can shut up 'like a box of matches' for easy transport. Betraying his Finnish origins, he says that it can be drawn either on a trailer by a car or on a sled by a snowmobile.

The piece also has a strong theoretical basis, forming part of his research into the concept of a 'minimum home', which draws on ideas first expressed at the second CIAM congress in Frankfurt in 1929.

When closed up, it measures 2.8 x 2 metres (9 feet 3 inches x 6 1/2 feet), with this latter dimension opening out to 3.5 metres (11 1/2 feet). It is 2.4 metres (7 feet 9 inches) high. Built with a wooden frame, it is clad in sandwich panels consisting of plywood treated with phenolic resin (a material more commonly used for truck floors) with polystyrene insulation in between. Integral shutters close the cabin up entirely for transport, and on arrival one simply swings down the door, opens the shutters and pushes out the inner section. The house stands on adjustable legs to take account of uneven ground.

The main space acts as a kitchen/living area, with all storage along one wall, and a table that can fold away, allowing the smaller sleeping unit to be pushed into it for transportation.

The prototype house weighs about 700 kilos (1,540 pounds) although Mossler & Doe believe that this could be halved if it goes into commercial production. Internally it uses colours reminiscent of the seasons in a Finnish forest and has a variety of windows to provide interesting views. Intended applications include a base on an island for fishing trips, a home for a forester or a first holiday home for a young couple.

Remoteness should not be a problem, since the intention is to use solar panels or a wind turbine to generate electricity. A cooker could be fuelled by kerosene, and a water tank included.

For Hedman this is just one of a series of experimental projects, of which others include Snail, aimed at urban environments, and the Shrewd Shed, prefabricated houses built for the Finnish housing exhibition in 2000. Such small projects have to carry a considerable theoretical weight, as Hedman is keen to discuss them in the context of both post-structuralism and critical hermeneutics. None of this, however, is likely to be visible to the casual observer, or indeed to the customers of Mossler & Doe, who will only see an exceedingly attractive holiday home.

Below and bottom: Eleva-
tions and sections showing
the cabin shut for transport
and open for use.

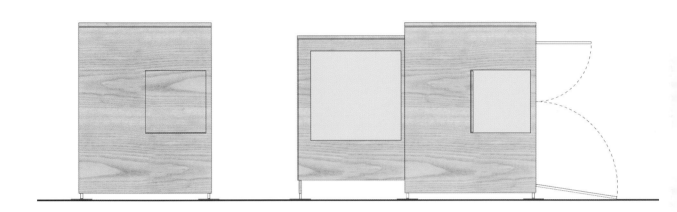

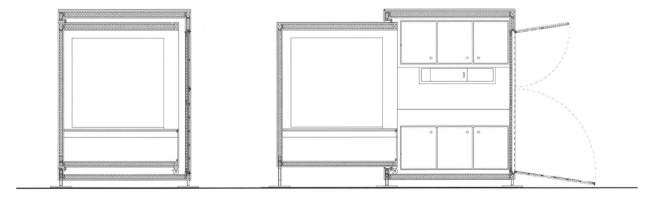

Opposite far left: With the shutters closed, the cabin presents an entirely impenetrable appearance.

Opposite near left: Windows have been positioned carefully to offer delightful views.

Below: Utterly at home in Finland's forests, the cabin should also appeal to Americans` love of movement and remote spots.

ADAM KALKIN
USA

PUSHBUTTON HOUSE

Shipping containers are uncompromising objects, but that has not prevented architects wanting to turn them into buildings. They have an industrial aesthetic, a quality of 'found' objects, and they are of course delightfully modular.

Architects are not the first to think of reusing containers. They have formed makeshift homes for the dispossessed wherever they stand unused and unguarded. And when they have been sold off inexpensively, business people looking for a robust enclosure have hacked and adapted them, with little thought for the aesthetic result.

In the US, at least, economics now favours their reuse. As Ann Guiney wrote in New York's *The Architect's Newspaper* on 22 June 2004, 'The abundance of shipping containers is a by-product of a trade imbalance that means that many more arrive in the United States than leave'. Typically, it cost shippers $900 to send back an empty container. So in today's throwaway society, they pile up like other debris. As a result, it is possible to buy a basic 6-metre (20-foot) container at prices starting at $2,000.

This makes them an appealing prospect for architects wanting to use them as building blocks in megastructures, and there are other practices, such as LOT-EK, who are interested in combining a few to make a desirable residence. Architect Adam Kalkin also became interested in their reuse, designing for example the art installation *A Collector's House* for the Shelburne Museum in Vermont in 2001. This housed three containers within an industrialized enclosure.

Kalkin has continued his association with both containers and the art world, and at the end of 2005 unveiled his latest project, the Pushbutton House, at the ArtBasel Miami fair. This was not, however, a purely theoretical project nor due for permanent installation in a gallery. It was a real project for a real client.

What makes Pushbutton House special is that it has no openings in the impenetrable exterior of the container. Instead, at the push of a button, it opens up hydraulically to reveal the interior. The excitement is like unwrapping a present, except that in this case you can wrap it again, and open it again, over and over.

Who would want to live in such a house? Although the idea is intriguing, it has definite implications for security and privacy. But Kalkin has found an ideal client, a company that is developing a resort in the Caribbean. As a sales office, it is equal to none. The company will take the house, put it on a deserted island, take potential clients there by boat, open up the house, give them coffee, talk about the development, and then close up the house and leave.

The house is, of course, fully transportable, as it has lost none of the robustness of the original container, and Kalkin says that several other developers in the region are showing interest. This is not however a lightweight solution. Each wall weighs a tonne, and there are four electric motors used for opening and closing. A computer controls these and all the valves. Inside, the container is fitted out as a six-room space.

Kalkin says that 'the house blossoms like a flower, turning space inside out. A box meant to hold things transforms into a place itself. Then, it folds closed as if it were ambivalent about its true nature.' More disturbingly, he adds, 'The Pushbutton House becomes an actor in the relationship between the viewer and the viewed to the point that it can swallow the visitor in its hydraulic jaws (thus disturbing the superior position that people usually enjoy over their living rooms).' Although this provides a nightmarish vision of recalcitrant prospects left stranded on a desert island inside a metal box, it only adds to the intriguing vision of the Pushbutton House. Like the coconut so often associated with such locations, it is hard and dark outside, but bright and sweet within.

Below: The impermeable
exterior of the container
unfolds to reveal the
spaces within.

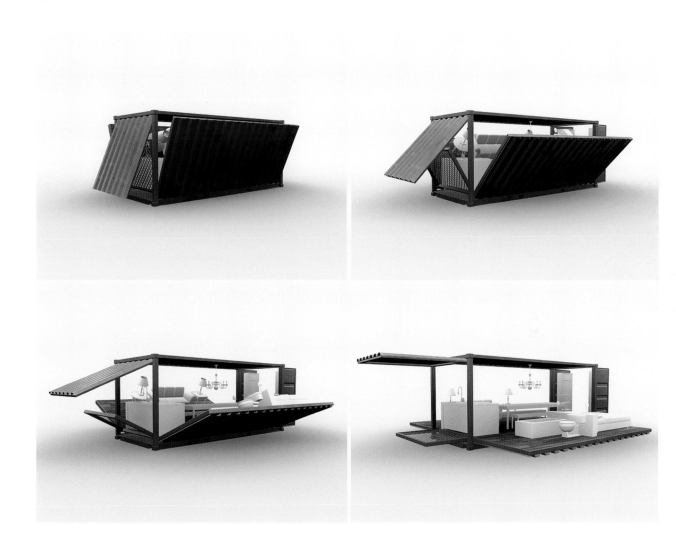

Below and opposite bottom: The fully furnished container in the process of opening (this page) and fully open (opposite).

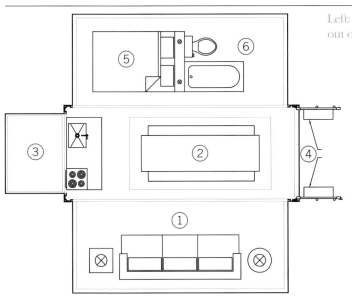

Left: Plan, showing the layout of the open container.

1: Living room;
2: Dining room;
3: Kitchen;
4: Book shelves;
5: Bedroom;
6: Bathroom

XS HOUSE

Jay Shafer is an architect who is offering one version of the American Dream. Build (or buy) a little wooden house with a pitched roof, that is well built and cosy. And if, or when, you decide you want to live somewhere else, just hitch it to the back of your car and tow it there.

Shafer evidently relishes the simple life and the idea of divesting himself of extraneous possessions, since the company that he runs grew out of his own passion, and he himself now lives in almost the smallest house that he offers. He worries about the environmental impact of having too big a house, and does not want to be surrounded by wasted space. His is a reaction against the conspicuous consumption in America that can extend to space as much as food or possessions – although evidently those possessions demand the space to put them in. As Shafer puts it, 'since 1997 I have been living in houses smaller than some people's bathrooms'.

The first house that Shafer built for himself he called Tumbleweed, and it had an area of just 9.3 square metres (100 square feet). It gave the name to his company, the Tumbleweed Tiny House Company, and it is a model that he still sells today.

But Shafer obviously felt he was rattling around in Tumbleweed, because in 2004 he sold it and built his current home, which is only 6.5 square metres (70 square feet). This he dubbed the Weebee or XS House, and it is almost the smallest house that he offers in his portfolio (one, called Elemeno, makes XS look positively palatial).

The XS weighs about 1,800 kilos (4,000 pounds) and measures 3.6 metres by 2.1 metres by 3.6 metres (11 feet by 7 feet by 11 feet), well within the dimensions allowed on any US road. But with rigorous planning, it offers everything needed, albeit in miniature (one thing you do not decide to do with a house on this scale is move the furniture around). It has a porch and an awning that can fold away for travel. Inside, there is a bathroom with a lavatory and shower, a kitchen with a double burner, a sofa and a desk space, a retractable table, several cupboards and shelves and, above the main space, a vented sleeping loft with room for a double bed.

Although Shafer will customize his buildings, there is a standard package. All his tiny houses have metal roofing, exposed stud interior walls and red oak flooring over insulation. There are proper windows. The smallest models come with profiled aluminium cladding and a cedar trim; others have pine board-and-batten cladding that can be painted any colour.

He says that his buildings are better constructed than so-called permanent buildings, as they have to withstand the rigours of road transport and being lifted into position. They have, therefore, been reinforced at the joints and all major connections are screwed rather than nailed.

Shafer's architecture is certainly not futuristic. As well as the pitched roofs, which are practical since they prevent his sleeping lofts becoming claustrophobic, he has a penchant for Gothic windows and turned balusters. But they are charming, and show how much can be done with very little.

He is not dogmatic, recognizing that while for some people his house may be a primary home, for others it will he a holiday home or granny flat or office. But he is passionate about his mission of 'showing America what a real house of viable proportions looks like' and is compiling a book, *Small by Design*, of houses that are less than 37 square metres (400 square feet) – although by Shafer's standards, of course, that would be recklessly extravagant.

Below: Floor plan.
1: Entrance;
2: Closet;
3: Desk;
4: Fold-out table;
5: Couch;

6: Shelves;
7: Kitchen;
8: Bathroom

Below left: Interiors are carefully appointed to make the most of the tiny space.

Below right: Profiled aluminium cladding is combined with a cedar trim.

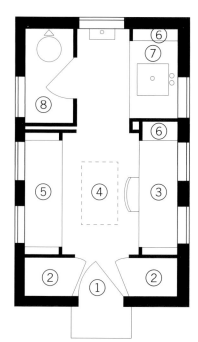

MIELE SPACE STATION

Although designed by a practice based in Rotterdam, the Miele Space Station is part of a movement that has grown up in the Netherlands largely centred around the 'Vinex' region of Leidsche Rijn near Utrecht. These are areas designated for urban expansion under the Fourth Document on Land Use Planning Extra (VINEX) of 1994. Like many such essentially suburban areas, Leidsche Rijn was lacking in many essential services. For example, research conducted in 2002 and published in *Leidsche Rijn Monitor* showed that the inhabitants of the area were not satisfied with the provision of shops.

In looking at the potential development of the area, the authorities responded to a train of alternative Dutch thought, the 'Parasite' movement, where 'Parasite' stands for 'Prototypes for Amphibious Readymade Advanced Smallscale Individual Temporary Ecological Houses'. Taken more widely, this represents a subversive kind of small-scale intervention,

providing low-cost and usually mobile elements that often involve recycled materials. Their mobility echoes the idea of mobile vans and other facilities that bring services to areas of dispersed population (think for instance, of the UK's now-vanishing tradition of mobile libraries). Artists and architects became involved in looking for solutions and an event in Leidsche Rijn called 'Parasite Paradise' was followed by a book of the same name, published by the Netherlands Architecture Institute.

2012 Architecten's Miele Space Station was included and sits comfortably in this new tradition. The practice is profoundly interested in the reuse of materials, and has developed a concept called 'Recyclicity' which is the subject of a long strand of information on its website. It has built a shoe shop for Duchi in Scheveningen that looks slick and contemporary but uses 90 per cent recycled materials – largely old timber and windscreens of defunct Audi 100 cars.

The Miele Space Station is built up from one of the most recognizable and rapidly obsolescent of consumer goods, the washing machine. There are five ring-like modules, each 60 centimetres (23 1/2 inches) wide, the width of a standard washing machine. Two people can easily lift one of the modules, and all five can be carried on the back of a truck. A module will roll through a standard door.

Assembled on the flatbed of a truck, the five modules together can act as a mobile office, making them productive even when travelling from one place to another. Once they reach the intended site, they can be combined and assembled in a number of ways. Uses have included a bar combined with an art-vending machine, a pavement café and a music shop/office/bar.

At the Parasite Paradise event, the space station became a mobile architects' office, acting as a research centre for the idea of using waste produced during the

construction of the area for other applications.

In addition to the five modules there are 'bridging pieces' that can be carried within the truck that transports the space station. Using these elements allows the construction of a structure up to 20 metres (65 1/2 feet) long that is entirely self-sufficient. It uses a wind turbine and solar panels to produce energy, and a solar cooker and solar boiler to generate heat. There are also systems for collecting water and composting waste.

Below left: The five modules plus bridging pieces can combine into a self-sufficient structure up to 20 metres (65 1/2 feet) long.

Bottom left: Fit-out can be in a number of manners, including this rather James Bond approach.

Below right: Built-in vegetable bowl – a new use for the porthole in a washing-machine door.

Bottom right: Each module is built up from dismembered elements of washing machines.

pPOD MOBILE THEATRE

Touring theatres have a history as long as theatre itself. Before the days of readily available transport, it made more sense for the theatre to come to its audience than the other way round. The Horse and Bamboo Theatre is in this tradition, and indeed originally travelled around the UK and Europe in a horse-drawn wagon, which is how it acquired its name. Its three actors staged, and still stage, a range of contemporary masked and puppet theatre, but it now operates from a base in Rossendale, Lancashire, in the north of England.

This does not, however, rule out the need for travel, as the theatre tours small towns and villages and puts on shows for groups of up to 35 people. To enable it to do this, it commissioned a travelling structure, the pPod, from Berlin-based practice magma. Could it have simply used a tent? Of course it could, but this custom-designed structure has a number of advantages.

It is fast to erect, and there is a theatricality to the process that in itself draws the crowds. And unlike a conventional tent it can stand on a hard surface, so it can be used as easily in a car park as in a large hall.

The theatre is constructed from six aluminium rectangles that are tilted round an imaginary axis. This results in a slightly drunken-looking shape, but one that is structurally stable. When the outer of two layers of fabric is stretched over it, it follows doubly curved hyperbolic paraboloids, despite the fact that there are no curved members supporting it. This stretched fabric provides both protection from the weather and longitudinal stability. Made of PVC-coated polyester sheeting, and in a strong red colour, this outer fabric has microscopic holes in it. These allow views through to the opaque silver-coloured inner fabric, but are small enough not to be penetrated by droplets of rainwater which, because of their surface tension, just run off the stretched fabric as if it were an umbrella.

The inner fabric, which hangs from curved inner members that also provide cross-stability, forms an opaque enclosure for the stage and auditorium. There is a floor system that consists of a frame of 10 x 10 centimetres (3 7/8 x 3 7/8 inches) rectangular hollow aluminium sections, fitted together and set in position by bracing cables. Counterweights are fitted to the edges of these frames when the theatre is used outside, to stop it being lifted by the wind. Film-faced plywood floor panels fit into the frame, and there is an entrance ramp, also of film-faced plywood, that makes wheelchair access possible. Both the benches and the stage are of foldable plywood.

Galvanized steel nodes join the elements of the aluminium frame. Because of the complex geometry, every one of these nodes is different. Originally it was thought that the aluminium tubes would be cut on a CNC router, but in the end they were cut and welded by hand. This meant that magma had to create a new detail for the nodes, with a steel sphere as the centre point, so that the steel pins could be cut perpendicular and would fit at every point of the sphere. The nodes are colour-coded to make assembly simpler. Artificial lighting is suspended between the inner and outer fabric, so that at night the tent glows.

The architects, working with two engineers from Buro Happold, have fulfilled the part of the brief that demanded 'a magical space and object', as well as creating a structure that the three actors can put up in 90 minutes. Travelling theatre has seen nothing like this; the little Lancashire theatre has created a benchmark against which others will be measured.

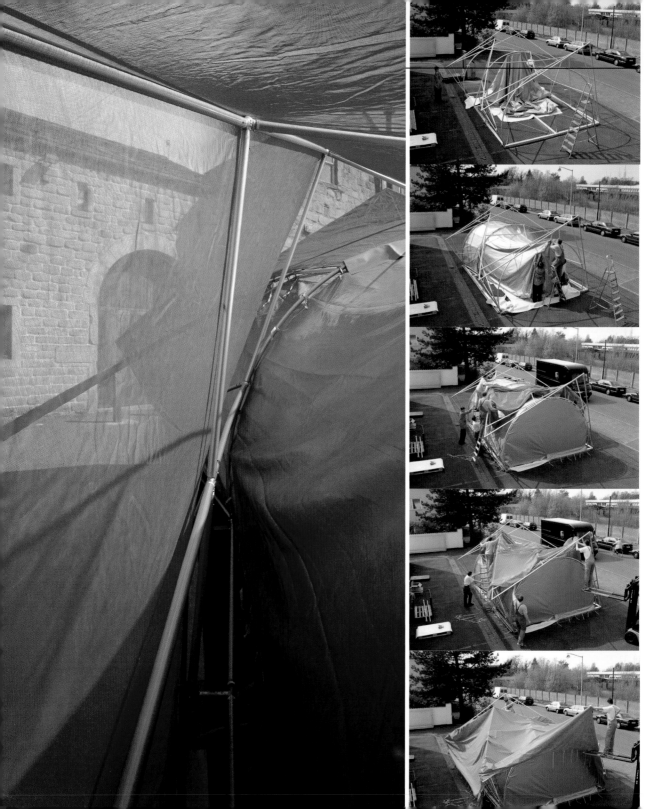

Opposite left: Tiny holes in
the outer fabric allow views
through while still keeping
out the rain.

Opposite right: Three
actors can erect the theatre
in just 90 minutes.

Below: The inner and
outer frames are the result
of clever engineering that
produces a drunken-look-
ing, but stable, lightweight
structure.

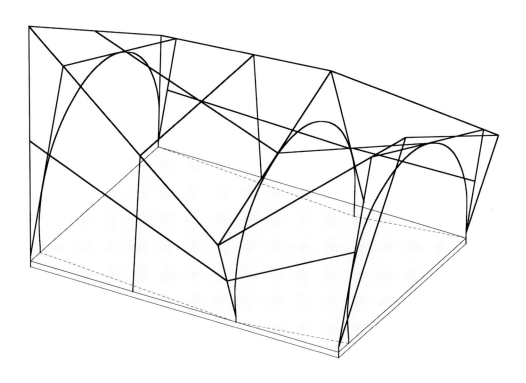

COMPACT LIVING

Left: Perriand's Refuge Bivouac, first installed on a mountain in 1929, was one of the first demonstrations of the feasibility of lightweight, movable shelter.

Below: The Cabanon at Roquebrune, France, was not merely a summer refuge for Le Corbusier but a laboratory for his ideas about dimensions and simplicity.

There can't be many log cabins that have been proposed for listing as UNESCO World Heritage Sites, but exactly that happened with one at Roquebrune Cap Martin in the south of France at the start of 2006. A modest-looking structure in an idyllic setting, its credentials for such an honour are not immediately obvious – until you realize that this is the famous Cabanon of Le Corbusier, where the colossus of modern architecture spent his summers, overlooking the beach off which he subsequently drowned in 1965.

Le Corbusier built his Cabanon in 1951 and, despite its unassuming exterior, it acted as a laboratory for his ideas. Measuring 3.66 metres x 3.66 metres x 2.26 metres high (12 feet x 12 feet x 7 1/2 feet), it was based on his Modulor dimensions, a system of proportions based on the human body.

For Le Corbusier, as well as being a delightful escape from the pressures of urban life, this was a follow-up to ideas from decades before – the new concepts of, ironically, urban living, developed by CIAM (Congrès Internationaux d'Architecture Moderne) formed in 1928 and culminating in the Athens Charter of 1933. These ideas of simplicity, of living in the smallest possible space and of prefabricating wherever possible, have continued to appeal both to architects who embrace Le Corbusier's legacy and to others who would deny his influence.

One of the earliest to take these ideas further was Le Corbusier's long-term collaborator Charlotte Perriand. She worked with Le Corbusier on the development of the 14-square-metre (150-square-foot) unit presented to CIAM in 1929 but, more importantly, she carried these ideas forward into practical application with first the weekend house, built up from a number of cells, and then the Refuge Bivouac. Intended for use on mountains, this latter was a lightweight aluminium structure that could be broken down into small enough elements

to be manhandled up the mountain. She and colleagues tested it by carrying it up Mont Joly to a height of 2,000 metres (6,000 feet). The four of them assembled it in four days, and then lived within the rigorously planned 8 square metres (86 square feet) for a further three days.

In this admirably realized project, one begins to see some of the contradictions that sneak in to the concept of small houses. Are they compact solutions offering low-cost living, or are they luxury second homes? The problem is that once a building becomes really small, there is only one way of living inside it – all the furniture and

fittings have to be planned, ideally designed as part of a whole, and you have to deny yourself any extraneous possessions. If you have chosen this way of living, it can be appealing, but if it has been forced on you as the only way that you can afford to live in our acquisitive society, then the effect is rather different.

So the most extreme of the realized projects here, the m-ch home by Horden Cherry Lee in collaboration with Haack + Höpfner (see page 136), has found its first incarnation as housing for students, who have not had the chance to accumulate many possessions. Described as 'business class' design, because of the

Below and bottom: Lucky
Drops House, Tokyo,
Japan, Atelier Tekuto and
Masahiro Ikeda, 2005. The
extremely narrow house
demonstrates the particular

skill of Japanese architects
in fitting homes on seem-
ingly impossible sites.

superb quality of materials, its appeal will be to the affluent and disciplined.

This is even truer of some of the projects shown here at the conceptual stage. While valuable in challenging our thinking about housing, they would certainly be unacceptable if imposed rather than chosen.

In contrast, the Katrina Cottage (see page 134) takes a far more conventional approach to housing, as befits its purpose – to provide inexpensive and relatively temporary homes for some of the families whose lives were devastated by Hurricane Katrina in the summer of 2005.

That building is relatively inexpensive, but there are also circumstances where people build tiny 'proper' houses that cost a considerable amount of money, because land itself is so scarce and so expensive. The prime country for this is Japan, where architects have risen to the challenge with some inventive designs. The house by Shuhei Endo

(see page 162) earns its place here not only for its size but also for being on such an improbable site. A similar level of inventiveness has been shown by Atelier Tekuto and Masahiro Ikeda in the long and very narrow Lucky Drops house in Tokyo, which has a section like a Gothic arch. In the Shinjuku-ku area of Tokyo, Atelier Bow-Wow has built a four-storey house above a narrow strip of pavement, raising it on stilts to allow pedestrians to continue passing underneath.

And in a country where the vast majority of houses are off-the-shelf kits, it is not surprising that imaginative designers have come up with compact and contemporary options, such as the 50-square-metre (538-square-foot) 9tubohouse by Boo-Hoo-Woo.com. In this, designers Makoto Koizumi and Makoto Masuzawa have used an attractive arrangement of sliding full-height glazing to create a small house that includes all the standard functions in a cleverly planned space. But where land is expensive,

Below: Casa de Pollo, Spain,
Santiago Cirugeda. The 30-
square-metre (322-square-
foot) house was designed to
demonstrate the possibilities
of compact social housing.

the more conventional solution is to build apartments,
and these lend themselves
to both prefabrication and
miniaturization. Exam-
ples include the brightly
coloured Spacebox student
apartments in Rotterdam
(see page 166) and the
Abito flats in Manchester,
England, designed by Building Design Partnership and
aimed at young profession-
als. In Catalonia, Spain, a
row blew up in 2005 when
the country's housing min-
ister, Maria Antonia Trujillo,
proposed the construction
of 30-square-metre (322-
square-foot) flats as a way
to tackle a housing crisis
compounded of a shortage
of property and high prices.
The regional government in
Catalonia refused to invest
in the idea, saying that such
flats were smaller than the
minimum acceptable area
in which one could live. In
response, architect Santiago
Cirugeda built a 30-square-
metre (322-square-foot)
Casa de Pollo (chicken
house) apartment entirely
from recycled materials as
a demonstration project,
arguing that potential
residents could build similar

places for themselves within
a week.

Small dwellings also have
a role to play away from
the pressures of city life. In
this situation it is probable
that more people hark
back to Thoreau's cabin at
Walden Pond than to Le
Corbusier, whose humble
dwelling now seems rather
incongruous in the swanky
setting of the Côte d'Azur.
Projects such as the woodland cabin of Robbrecht
en Daem Architecten (see
page 168) certainly look
back to this rustic lineage,
although as internationally
distinguished architects
their ascetic isolation is only
temporary.

MARIANNE CUSATO
NEW ORLEANS, USA

KATRINA COTTAGE

There is nothing revolutionary about this cheerful little yellow-painted house, designed by Marianne Cusato of New York, but that is exactly the point. It is not meant for people who are ready to embrace experiment and adventure, but for the people in and around the southern US city of New Orleans whose homes were devastated by Hurricane Katrina at the end of August 2005. The Katrina Cottage was designed to give them back some dignity and help them to begin the painful process of rebuilding their lives – and their homes.

As architectural historian and cultural commentator Witold Rybczynski has written, 'I've never lost my house in a flood, but I would imagine that "cute" would beat "cutting edge" every time.'

Cusato drew up the idea for the cottage as an alternative to the trailers that FEMA, the Federal Emergency Management Agency, was putting people into as a 'temporary solution'. As we all know, such temporary solutions are liable to last much longer than anticipated. So Cusato's proposal was for a compact, inexpensive home that could form a temporary residence and then could be expanded or built around when more funds and time became available. There was an important precedent from nearly a century before, when San Francisco built 6,000 two-room wooden 'cottages' or 'shacks' to provide better temporary housing than the tents that were the first offer after the 1906 earthquake. Many of these cottages were incorporated into permanent residences.

Launched at the International Builders' Show in January 2006, the Katrina Cottage was designed to be the same size as a FEMA trailer, with a floor area of 28.8 square metres (308 square feet), measuring 4.3 metres x 6.7 metres (14 feet x 22 feet), plus a 2.5-metre (8-foot) porch. Based on a Mississippi coastal cottage, it manages to fit in a living–dining space, a small kitchen, a full-size bathroom and a bedroom with two sets of bunk beds and storage underneath. There is even space for a closet.

The house was built of timber frame with fibre-cement siding and a tin roof. Cusato paid particular attention to details such as the windows, and there is heating and air conditioning. The aim was to give a feeling of quality. Built in just three weeks for the show, and trucked in, the prototype showed what could be done quickly, although Cusato said that the construction method could vary.

A later variant, Katrina Cottage II, pushed the floor area up to 60 square metres (650 square feet) and added a second bedroom. Both versions are raised above the ground, to allow for construction on a flood plain. They are also, unsurprisingly, intended to resist hurricanes.

The Katrina Cottage has attracted criticism both from those who feel that its design is too conservative and from those, such as Rybczynski, who welcome the concept but feel that, at around $1,000 a square metre ($100 a square foot), it is too expensive.

Even enthusiasts for the design worried that it would not pass government hurdles, precisely because these only pay for temporary accommodation after disasters and the Katrina Cottage had too great an air of permanence. But in April 2006, Louisiana senator Mary Landrieu, as part of a new package of spending nationally and locally to mitigate the after-effects of Katrina, doubled an allocation of $600 million to spend on a pilot programme of Katrina Cottages, to $1.2 billion.

Nor does it stop there. California, for example, is looking seriously at the cottages as part of its forward planning for when – not if – the next massive earthquake happens along the San Andreas fault.

Below left: Based on a Mississippi coastal cottage, the Katrina Cottage is designed to look like a home to be proud of.

Bottom left: Cusato's design contrasts with the squalor of sites full of FEMA trailers.

Below right: A porch plays a key part in this design for a hot and humid part of the country.

Bottom right: Inside there are all the facilities one would expect, albeit in a compact space.

MICRO-COMPACT HOME (M-CH)

British architect Richard Horden is still a partner in the London practice Horden Cherry Lee, but is also now professor of architecture and design at the University of Munich, and it is appropriate that students there should be the first to benefit from his latest innovation. Called the micro-compact home (m-ch), it is designed to solve housing shortages in as agreeable and effective a way as possible. Even Horden, an advocate of abolishing wasted space as much as other wasted resources, would not expect such a tiny enclosure to form a permanent home. So the intended use is by students and other birds of passage more concerned with having a roof over their heads than with generous dimensions.

Horden claims that the design is based on the concept of the Japanese tea house, although some may be reminded more of the capsule hotel. Measuring just 2.6 metres (8 1/2 feet) in each dimension, it nevertheless manages to include all the essentials for life, on two levels. This Horden achieves by having a full-height entrance, shower and kitchen area, and a sunken dining area with a fold-down double bed above it. Storage is both beneath the floor and behind the dining area. Materials are aluminium, perspex and epoxy-coated OSB (oriented strand board).

The trick for living in such a tiny space is that everything is purpose-made and fitted in, but Horden envisages a range of cubes with different functions. The shower and lavatory doubles as an entrance lobby where students can divest themselves of their snowy clothes. Dripping water will drain away through the outlet grille of the shower. There is an integral sound system and two flat-screen television monitors with broadband connection. The kitchen has a double radiant hob and a microwave oven plus a fridge/freezer. Living is not, therefore, austere.

Windows incorporate privacy blinds, and lighting consists of LED low-temperature technology, avoiding the danger of overheating on summer evenings. The cube is highly insulated, so that energy use should be low, and there is potential for placing photovoltaic panels on both the mast and the flat roof.

With such a small area, there is no need for conventional rainwater drainage. Instead rain can run off the flat roof and down behind the rainscreen cladding to the ground.

The tiny house works because every detail has been considered so carefully, and because everything is well made and of the highest quality. Doors and drawers open and shut with the reassuring clunk that one gets from a top-of-the-range car.

The idea of a living cube is not entirely new. For example, German practice Sturm und Wartzeck came up with a prototype of a rotatable housing cube in 1998. With high levels of insulation and photovoltaic panels, it is nearly self-sufficient in energy. This effectiveness is increased by the building having one highly glazed façade and being able to rotate to face either towards or away from the sun, depending on the time of year. This does, however, mean that the cube is seen as an object on its own in the landscape, whereas part of Horden's cleverness lies in the fact that he has thought of a number of ways of combining the units.

In Munich, where there is a terrible shortage of student housing, the student housing authority, with sponsorship from telephone company O_2, has built the O_2 Village, a two-level cluster of six inhabited units plus an experimental one. Horden, in collaboration with Munich-based Haack + Höpfner Architekten, uses 150-millimetre (6-inch) steel tubes to create the support structure, and envisages everything from a one-off house to a multi-storey complex. For example, he sees potential for a 'tree village', 15 metres (49 feet) high, of 30 of the micro-compact homes surrounding a central lift-core and stairs. An internal ring of vertical

Left: Inside, high-quality finishes make a liveable space even with the bed folded down.

Below: A single micro-compact home can provide an elegant refuge in the midst of the natural environment.

Opposite top: At Munich University, several units have been combined to form a student village.

Opposite below: With the bed folded away there is space for eating, working or relaxing.

service 'reeds', would supply power and water.

Reeds are also a reference point in the reed huis collaboration with Dutch artist Marijke de Goey, intended for a reed-based landscape. Here the masts are multiplied beyond the purely functional to form an enclosing structure that echoes both the surrounding landscape and de Goey's sculptural interests. Intended uses are as accommodation for those on sailing or skating holidays, or as rural retreats.

In contrast, the Golden Cube would be one of a series of unconnected units, intended to provide relatively inexpensive accommodation for holiday-makers in that most rapacious of cities, Venice, Italy. The cubes would sit in the lagoon, stabilized by vertical piles on either side and accessible only by boat. There would be platforms on two sides, and a canopy above the entrance with photovoltaic cells providing electricity. A solar pump would circulate lagoon water for

cooling, and all waste would be stored and removed by boat. In keeping with the baroque opulence of the city, the aluminium exterior would be anodized in a gold colour.

Although not intended as 'mobile homes', the cubes could relatively easily be moved to other locations. With a cost of only about £30,000 ($55,000), the m-ch homes are already attracting interest from other places with housing shortages. London, for instance, has shown interest in using them to provide key-worker housing. Another forthcoming project is for a ski village, and in preparation Horden has adapted the design to include an external lockable drawer for storing skis and ski boots.

The Munich students took a few weeks to adapt to living in the houses, and then professed themselves very happy with them, asking to extend their stay from a semester to a year. The girls, in particular, liked the sense of security and the fact that they did not have to live

with other people's mess. With a laundry and a bar nearby, the students were not relying on their tiny homes for every need, but having moved in at a time in life when they naturally have very few possessions, it will be interesting to discover if they will have learnt habits of clutter-free living that will carry through to a taste for compact living once their lives become more complicated.

Below left: The Golden
Cube could provide holiday
accommodation in Venice.

Below: Section and plan of
a cube.
1: Terrace;
2. Entrance/shower;
3. Storage;
4. Dining area;

5. Kitchen;
6. Sliding door;
7. PVC inner lining;
8. Aluminium tube;
9. Overhead double bed

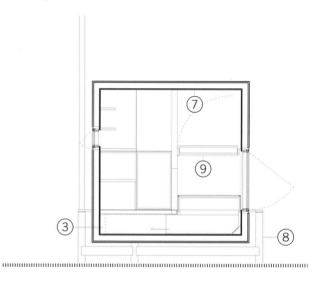

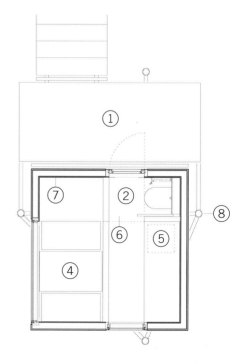

Left: Model showing how the tiny homes could be combined to form a 'tree village' 15 metres (49 feet) high, with vertical 'reeds' supplying essential services.

UBALDO GARCIA TORRENTE
LA TORRERA, SPAIN

CAMPING CABINS

With much of the environment of Spain degraded as the result of the tourism industry, it is refreshing to see a development where tourism is helping to drive regeneration. At La Torrera near Huelva, one of the least picturesque towns of Andalucía, old mine workings have been re-landscaped to create a nature reserve with a water-sports centre that will attract campers all year round. It includes 13 small cabins designed by local architects' practice Ubaldo García Torrente. Aimed at visitors who want more protection from the elements than a tent can provide, and slightly more creature comforts, the cabins are strung along the waterfront facing south to southwest. They have a self-contained form slightly reminiscent of a US mailbox and use modern materials to create dwellings that are both charming and unobtrusive.

Steel-framed, the cabins sit on concrete platforms that project over the water, and the whole of the southern façade is an up-and-over door that opens to a balcony. The roof overhangs on this side to provide some shade.

Walls are of sandwich-panel construction, with polyurethane insulation contained between an outer layer of PVF2-coated aluminium and an inner face of enamelled particleboard. The roofs consist of two sheets of galvanized steel with insulation between them.

Internally, the layout is simple and basic. A double bunk, accessed by a ladder, projects over a small lavatory and kitchen at the north end of the cabin. Running down from these is a long shelf on which two children can sleep end to end. During the day this can provide seating with a space in front of it for eating simple meals.

Most definitely holiday accommodation, rather than a compact solution for permanent living, these cabins provide a way of spending time with nature that is unadorned but in no way makeshift or ramshackle.

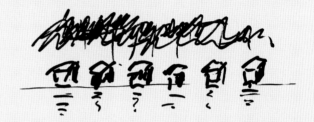

Opposite: Initial sketch of
the cabins.

Below: Sitting in a row on
the water's edge, the cabins
allow visitors to be in touch
with the environment.

Below: Entrance to the cabins is from the rear.

Bottom: Old mine workings have been landscaped to create a delightful nature reserve.

Opposite top: Site plan showing the cabins on the water's edge, with communal facilities set behind.

Opposite bottom: Plan and sections of a cabin.

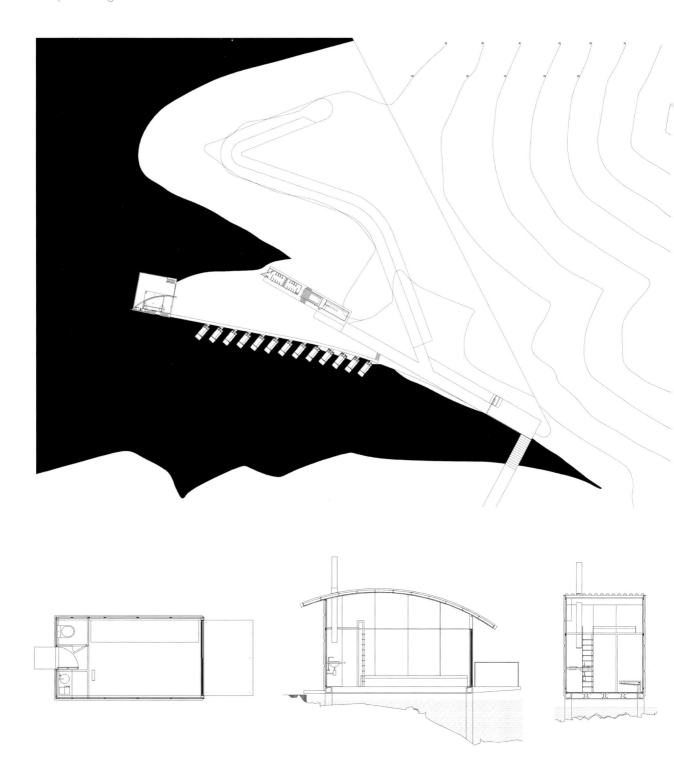

BRECKENRIDGE PERFECT COTTAGE

Go to the website of Breckenridge Recreational Park Trailers, which turns out 15 units a day and bills itself as the 'largest park-model-specific manufacturing plant in the world', and you will see something rather incongruous. It is asking visitors whether they would be interested in buying a Breckenridge Perfect Cottage and what price they would be prepared to pay.

Customer research is always laudable, but what appears odd here is that whereas all the other models on offer have a retro, homestead-like look, the Perfect Cottage is a piece of slick Modernism in which nobody could imagine themselves as a pioneer of the covered-wagon persuasion or slip comfortably into a rocking chair.

It is the brainchild of Christopher C. Deam, an architect and furniture designer who spent his youth shuttling between the west and east coasts of America and therefore is attracted by the idea of mobility. He wanted to 'crack the code' of prefab and to use RV

(recreational vehicle) technology to create something modern, for which he felt there was a hunger.

He deliberately went to Breckenridge because of its size. His revolutionary solution still fits into the category of RV, which means is that it is no larger than 37 square metres (400 square feet) and so does not count as a building. That in turn means that in most states it can be placed on rural land without a permit.

The primary use that Deam envisages for his design is as a weekend or holiday home. Buyers will get a large living room-cum-kitchen, complete with Corian worktop (not usual RV territory), a full-size bathroom and a bedroom. What they will also get, which most RV users do not, is a superlative view, since one complete wall is glazed, with four sets of sliding aluminium-framed doors. Since this makes the interior somewhat exposed, there are also sliding wood louvred panels that will cover these doors externally for solar control,

security – and privacy. In fitting with the smart aesthetic, the 'basic' model comes complete with track lighting and dark timber cladding.

Add-on extras include sunscreens, awnings and a deck – the last an attractive option to extend the home into an outdoor living space, easily reached through the glazed doors. The box-like form, with slightly rounded corners, reeks of quality and metropolitan sophistication.

This is not the first time that Deam has become involved with the RV market, since he has previously designed interiors for Airstream trailers, but it is his first venture into creating the complete package. He has had to address issues such as making the glass wall sturdy enough to travel at high speed on national roads, and also ensuring quality in such a rapid production process. If Breckenridge's survey of its potential customers produces positive results, there should be some much more stylish RVs popping up around the United States.

Below left: The cottage is designed to be transported by truck.

Below right: Slick design and extensive glazing are a world away from most RVs.

Bottom: Plan of the Perfect Cottage.

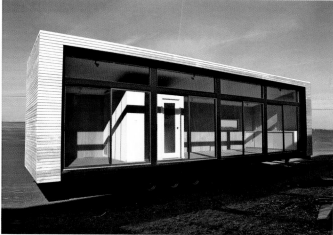

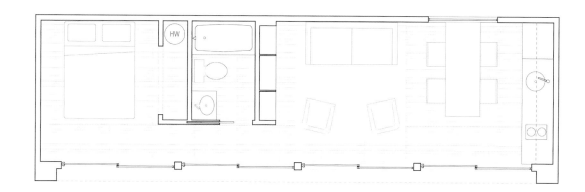

FISHCAMP

Fish Camp is a clever name for a cleverly designed kit assembly building designed by Rocio Romero, a California-trained architect who is putting much of her effort into prefabricated houses. She has two ranges, the LV series, intended for use as either a permanent residence or a vacation home, and the Camp series, intended entirely for recreational use. This could either be in a permanent position, or could be relocated every few years.

Fish Camp is the smaller of the two Camps (the other is Base Camp) and measures 3.7 metres x eight metres (12 feet x 26 feet). It can be configured as one space, or can include a small bathroom or kitchenette if it is to operate as a single self-contained living space.

The lines are clean and simple, and Romero is proud of the fact that two people should be able to assemble it in just two days. The secret lies in the use of SIPs (structural insulated panels), which in this case have a galvalume (alumini-um-zinc alloy coated steel) outer face, and a prepared timber sheathing inner face, with a layer of expanded polystyrene insulation between. With holes already pre-drilled, the only tool needed for assembly is a power screwdriver. If the building is to sit on permanent foundations, Romero has even built in some flexibility in the structure to take account of tolerances in the positioning of the foundations. The roof panels, like the walls, provide both the exterior surface and a primed interior ready for painting.

Romero's design includes access tunnels for cabling and points for plumbing, so that the building needs little more than connection to services. Windows and sliding doors, again designed to fit snugly and with good insulation properties, come as part of the package, and there is even an outdoor shower.

Unlike many American prefabricated homes, which try to disguise their origins with chintzy details, Fish Camp looks like exactly what it is – and is better for it. The straightforward metal exterior sets off the generous glazing. The roof, with a shallow single pitch, rises to the front of the building, so that run-off will occur at the back. This simple structure, with carefully thought-out details but no pretensions, would be an excellent building in which to holiday. It may be time to learn to fish.

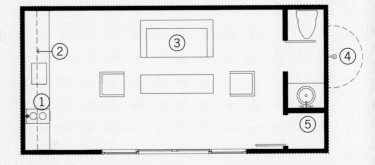

Opposite: Plan.
1: Kitchenette;
2: Line of cabinets overhead;
3: Living/dining area;
4: Outdoor shower;
5: Water heater

Below: The uncompromising appearance of Fish Camp is a reflection of the simple construction system.

Bottom left: Sliding doors open onto a deck.

Bottom right: The structural insulated panels are finished on the inside with timber sheathing.

MICRODWELLINGS

Austerity doesn't get much more extreme than in the Microdwellings devised by Danish artists' collective N55, which can, as the organization says 'be constructed by anybody who knows how to weld'. Their irregular polyhedral form, made up of hexagons and squares, is supported on a tripod of short legs on pads, with the idea that the impact on their surroundings should be minimized. Although when considered as a straight option they would only suit a user with no requirement for comfort, privacy or even sanitation, they are only a starting point for one of the group's developments, all of which reflect its serious concerns with personal property and finding alternative ways of living.

Indeed, the shape is reminiscent, on a smaller scale, of the Spaceframe, a structure on a raft in Copenhagen harbour that the group built in 1992 and has lived on ever since. That has a floor space of only 20 square metres (215 square feet), making it pretty

micro itself. In contrast, the Microdwellings, which can also float or be suspended, can be assembled to form a larger conglomeration, with units of several sizes. At the time of writing, there were plans for the construction of a 'Space on Earth Station' for an exhibition in London made up from the units, offering a possible way of living as the planet becomes less and less able to tolerate a 'natural' form of existence.

But N55 has put thought into the way that a single Microdwelling could work, creating an interior with a shelf that can be both table and bed, and a chair that echoes the form of the dwelling itself. People who want to live closely together could put their dwellings next to each other, or even join them, and as families expanded they could simply add more units.

Founded in 1966 and latterly consisting of a pair of members, Ion Sørvin and Ingvil Aarbakke (tragically, Aarbakke died of cancer in 2005 at the age of only 35),

N55 is dedicated to the concept of common ownership and of eliminating personal possessions. Projects range from Land, an accumulation of plots of land in many countries that offer free and open access to all, to 'small truck', which is exactly what it says, a (largely) human-powered truck for moving small amounts of goods around cities. In keeping with N55's ideals, the construction methods are freely available, materials are as basic as possible (for instance, rubber doormats are used as bumpers), and as many spin-off ideas as possible are envisaged.

More closely allied to the idea of dwelling is the Snail Shell System, which received considerable publicity when Aarbakke rolled it through the streets of the northern English city of Leeds in 2002. A stunted cylinder of polypropylene, it can be rolled from one place to another on removable caterpillar tracks. An oar clipped to one side is an indication of the number of environments considered, since it can float, sit on the

ground or be buried. Three mooring points are included. There are only three intrusions into the main form – an entrance, an air inlet and a bilge pump. This last can also work as a vacuum cleaner or, with the addition of a hose, as a shower. A cylindrical storage box doubles, when empty, as a lavatory. And a layer of insulating foam on one side also provides a mattress.

Although a cleverly worked out idea, this Snail Shell makes the Microdwelling seem almost decadent in its home comforts. But by asking questions about how we live and what is necessary, N55 holds up a mirror to the consumerism and hidebound thinking that pollutes the relationship that most of us have with our homes.

Below: N55 envisages com-
bining the Microdwellings
to form a community.

Bottom: Ingvil Aarbakke rolled the Snail Shell System through city streets to show how transportable basic accommodation could be.

Below: A stool and a shelf that can double as a bed make an individual Microdwelling almost habitable.

Opposite top: A skylight and a porthole bring light into the Microdwelling.

Opposite bottom: Standing alone, a single Microdwelling has a presence that is greater than its size.

TURNON

Have you ever felt like a hamster, trapped in its wheel? If Vienna-based practice AllesWirdGut had its way, this experience could become even more familiar. It has developed a prototype for a house which, although the architects define it as '100 per cent art project', is also intended to raise some serious questions about the way that we use space.

Called turnOn, the project consists of five modules that can be installed in any combination within an existing space – or even outdoors, the architects suggest boldly. Each of these is a wheel-shaped cylinder, and although the external dimensions are all the same, internally each one is different. The idea is that whichever function you wish to use is on the floor (the architects have not yet found a way to overcome gravity), and you can replace it with a turn of a wheel. So, for instance, having sat in your chair to relax in the evening, you can, with a spin of the wheel, dismiss the chair and replace it with a bed. There

is even a 'wet cell' incorporating a lavatory, shower and bath. Disconcertingly, this means that when you are in the bath, the lavatory will be upside down above you. The plumbing works by a suction system, similar to that used in aeroplanes.

The practice (its name means 'all goes well') is by no means purely theoretical, with an impressive portfolio ranging from one-off houses to civic buildings. So, although it does not expect turnOn to be built as such, nor is the project a mere folly. Instead, the architects see it as a manifesto, a challenge to an industry that it believes should be embracing manufacturing more wholeheartedly and acting more like the car industry.

In contrast, they say, 'housing still deals with the same parameters as it did a thousand years ago – we still live on plane floors, surrounded by corners – rigid configurations of given living set-ups that restrict our individuality – our desire to express ourselves is kept small within stiff white walls

and standardized educated mind cages.'

AllesWirdGut has built two sets of prototypes, each 3 metres (10 feet) in diameter and 1 metre (3 feet 3 inches) deep. The first, weighing about 300 kilos (660 pounds), was handmade from insulation, a wooden framework, a steel base and a fibreglass and resin skin. It is turned by human muscle-power. The second version was machine-made, in MDF with a high-gloss finish. Weighing much more, at 1,200 kilos (2,640 pounds), it is turned by an electric engine. And the practice has also produced detailed instructions for transport and assembly – determined to ensure that 'all goes well'.

Right: Prototypes have been built for exhibition.

Below: The wet cell incorporates a shower, bath and lavatory.

Overleaf: Human muscle power is sufficient to turn the lighter prototypes.

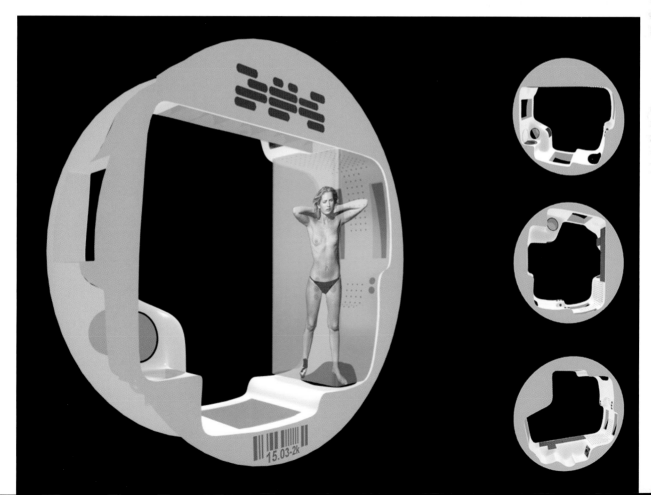

ROTORHAUS

Most houses are, by definition, largely wasted space. Bedrooms are mostly deserted outside sleeping hours, and bathrooms and kitchens are only occupied for a few hours a day at most. In the Rotorhaus, Luigi Colani has not entirely eliminated this redundancy, but he has at least minimized it. Designed for German housebuilder Hanse Haus, and so far only a prototype, it is far more imaginative than anything else that the builder produces.

Colani, who is based in Switzerland and described as 'a sculptor, painter, flight engineer, technical designer and city planner by occupation but aerodynamicist, 3-D and form philosopher from passion', designs rounded organic forms. Indeed, he has written: 'I am going to pursue Galileo Galilei's philosophy: my world is also round.' So the Rotorhaus, although almost square in external shape, albeit with rounded edges, is right up his street.

The idea is that the main area is living space, and then there is a 'rotor', a round electronically controlled form in the corner, that serves a tripartite function. At night, the sleeping area is brought round; at bath time the unit with bath and wash-basin comes into play, and at meal times the kitchen unit rotates into place. All these elements can be of minimal size since they 'borrow' space from the main living room. The bedroom, for example, consists simply of a bed, suspended above storage space.

In appearance, internally, the Rotorhaus is like a throwback to futuristic visions of the middle part of the twentieth century, with generous use of injection-moulded white plastic. But the idea, to create relatively generous living space for a couple within a footprint that is only 6 x 6 metres (19 1/2 x 19 1/2 feet), is a clever one.

The only separate elements are a lavatory and the entrance area. In keeping with the not-quite-square nature of the exterior, windows have rounded corners and there is one porthole window that has a tripartite division rather like a ventilator or the plan of the rotor or, less prosaically, the ancient Celtic *triskele* that divides land and air and water.

With its own deck, the house, from outside, looks like a desirable addition to a neighbourhood or the kind of investment that generous parents might make for their offspring and place in the garden.

There are evident drawbacks that would have to be overcome, not least the dependence on technology. What happens if there is a power cut? Or everything gets stuck? Or even gets a mind of its own, and whizzes round in the manner of a Feydeau farce? One can imagine the adulterous hausfrau tucking her lover away in the bedroom, while acting out the picture of domestic bliss and preparing a meal.

These are all reasons why the house may not take off and it is reasonable to wonder whether Hanse Haus, with its dedication to more conventional techniques, to quality workmanship and consultation with its clients, intends it as much more than a talking point. But it is, at the very least, a valuable contribution to the debate about the future of housing.

Below: The house uses
space as effectively as
possible.

Below:
Plan of the Rotorhaus.
1: Motor;
2: Bedroom;
3: Kitchen;
4: Bathroom;

5: Living room;
6: Entrance;
7: Terrace;
8: WC

Opposite top: The bath-
room and bedroom units in
the rotor.

Opposite bottom: The tim-
ber-clad Rotorhaus is more
elegant outside than inside.

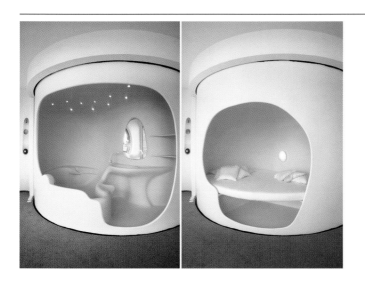

ROOFTECTURE S

There are plenty of small houses around, but few that squeeze into sites as unpromising as the one that Shuhei Endo Architecture Institute has exploited in Kobe, Japan. This is a narrow strip of land on a steep hillside above a railway line that one would automatically dismiss as unbuildable. Situated against a retaining wall, the footprint of the house is only 1.5 metres (5 feet) wide at one end, increasing to a scarcely generous 4 metres (13 feet) at the other end. It is 20 metres (65 1/2 feet) long.

On this Endo has constructed one of his Rooftecture series, which uses a continuous metal strip to enclose a space in terms of walls and roof. Endo himself has defined it as 'architectonic conduct in which continuous strips of roof/wall are identified as a sole means of creating architectural spaces. Using these continuous strips of roof/wall was an attempt to create versatile spaces without being restricted to further propagation of monotonous spaces.'

At Kobe, this 'rooftecture' in fact just describes the upper element, a wedge both in plan and section, which sits on top of a more rectilinear rendered white form. But the house is impressive both because of and despite the constraints of the site.

It was not possible to impose any lateral load on the retaining wall, which runs at a height of between 5 metres (16 1/2 feet) and 8 metres (26 feet) behind the site. Instead, the house is supported on five vertical columns. This leaves a gap between it and the retaining wall, filled at upper-floor level by a timber deck used for access and reached by a staircase down from the road above (it is this road that the retaining wall supports). The metal cladding, running horizontally on the railway side and vertically on the road side, is also used internally, forming the ceiling to the main, upper space. The front of the wedge is entirely glazed at the thin end, and houses the kitchen. Behind this is the living area, with the bedroom at the back. Windows

at the 'front' of the building are positioned to draw the eye beyond the railway below to the sea. Those on the other side give views of the intriguing structure of the retaining wall.

A stairwell cut out of the living-room floor leads down to the lower-floor, occupied by the bathroom and lavatory, and also by a contemporary interpretation of a *doma*, a traditional Japanese room that would have had an earth floor and served as a kind of lobby-cum-kitchen-cum-workroom. This in turn leads out to a courtyard at the wider end of the site. Overshadowed by the building above, and facing onto the railway line, this is not the most idyllic of spaces. But to have created any outside space at all is simply the last in a list of remarkable achievements, on a site where lesser architects would not have imagined that they could build at all.

Below left: Plan of the main, upper floor, and cross-section of the building and site.
1: Eating area;
2: Kitchen;
3: WC;
4: Living area;
5: Bedroom;
6: Entrance deck;
7: Courtyard

Below right: The kitchen occupies the thin end of the wedge.

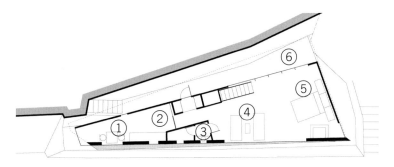

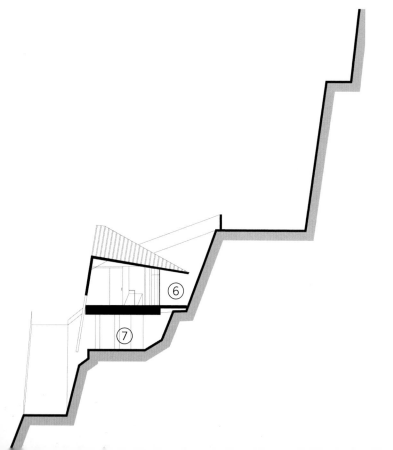

Below: Wrapped in metal
and positioned against a retaining wall, the main part of
the house has windows high
enough to look out beyond
the railway line beneath.

SPACEBOX

In Delft and Utrecht in the Netherlands, accumulations of brightly coloured boxes, stacked three high, have sprung up to provide student accommodation. In Eindhoven, just to prove that it is possible to be more restrained visually, a similar complex has been constructed all in white. And another is planned for Hilversum, in more pastel hues.

These structures are the brainchild of Mart de Jong of De Vijf in Rotterdam. They are highly insulated pre-fabricated studio apartments, which can be stacked on top of each other with no extra supporting structure. Placed simply on a set of concrete pads, they are accessed from behind by walkways that in turn are reached by staircases at either end of the development. The use of composites previously employed in the aircraft industry makes the boxes lightweight while allowing the incorporation of the insulation that gives them such good thermal and acoustic performance. With the inclusion of some vertical steel elements in the walls, the boxes are strong enough to be supported directly on each other, up to three storeys high, and, at only 2,500 kilos (5,500 pounds), can be lifted into place by a relatively small crane. The students who occupy them get a living space totalling 17 square metres (182 square feet), and incorporating a kitchen, bathroom and storage space. They are fully fitted out, and the front elevation is all glazed, including an opening door with a Juliet balcony.

Wall and roof panels have a total thickness of 8.8 centimetres (3 1/2 inches) and are built up from a range of materials, including a laminate surface, insulation and a fire barrier. Floors, similar but with the addition of some timber beams, can support a load of 175 kilos per square metre (308 pounds per square yard). Depending on the orientation – this is one of the disadvantages of single-aspect living – an external sunblind may also be needed, and can be fitted.

Amid all the futuristic designs that one sees, what is impressive about this is that it has actually been built and is being used. Malvina Reynolds, in her song 'Little Boxes', written in 1962 and made famous by Pete Seeger, was of course writing about suburban homes but seems oddly prescient in her description of boxes in different colours. These, however, may all look the same, but are certainly not made of 'ticky-tacky'. Students should be grateful for the Spacebox, which provides inexpensive living in a distinctive manner.

Below, left to right: Units arriving two at a time in Utrecht are lifted into place directly on top of the ones below, and quickly form a colourful array of housing.

Below centre: White units in Eindhoven, complete with Juliet balconies.

Bottom right: At Delft, as in all the developments, access is via staircases at the ends of the blocks.

WOODLAND CABIN

Rough-and-ready is the term that one would most easily apply to the tiny woodland cabin that Belgian architects Robbrecht en Daem Architecten have constructed in the woods of southern Flanders. Has some primitive woodsman hacked it out of tree trunks with his axe? That is the first impression that this organic, dumpy-looking structure gives.

In fact, its scaly exterior is made up from an entirely regular series of wooden blocks, joined together by dowels. It consists of two curved lobes with two angled glazed doors at the front, opening onto a wooden platform that leads off through the woods on a series of raised timber paths. The roof is also of timber, with a covering of peat.

This is the hilly and surprisingly wild countryside of the Flemish Ardennes – a tough environment with lots of ups and downs, plenty of mud, and scenery that is constantly changing and yet formless in a way that can make orientation difficult.

The little cabin is in keeping with its surroundings. Look down on it from the hill above, and on a drizzly day you would scarcely know it was there. The situation is clever; it commands not only a gentle path but it is also next to a pond that gives some opening and focus to the otherwise rather formless surroundings.

The idea is that amenities are kept to a minimum with just a bed, small table, two chairs and a stove – wood-burning, naturally. All other activities take place either on the external platform, or in the wider woodland. There is a slightly hobbit-like self-consciousness to the extreme ungainliness of the wooden furniture, but it fits with the ethos of the project, which turns its back in every way on urban living. The practice is better known for large international arts projects – for example, the Bojmans Van Beuningen Museum in Rotterdam, the Netherlands, and the current remodelling of London's Whitechapel Art Gallery. There is no way that you could get yourself sufficiently spruced up in this little cabin to attend a private view at these or any other venue – and that is a large part of its appeal.

Below: Cleverly sited beside a pond, with raised paths emanating from it, the wooden cabin with its peat roof blends easily into its surroundings.

Bottom left: The deck provides essential extra living space, to which the handmade furniture can be carried out.

Bottom right: Wooden blocks, connected by dowels, make up the walls.

EXTRA SPACE

Left: George Bernard
Shaw's revolving writing
hut, Shaw's Corner, Ayot
St Lawrence, UK. Built on
castors, it could be rotated
to follow the sun.

Below left: Balloon for Two,
Vienna, Austria, Haus-Rucker-Co, 1967. The suspended
ball allowed the architects to
sit 'outside' their office.

Below right: Yellow Heart,
also by Haus-Rucker-Co,
comprised a pulsating
bubble inside an inflated
capsule.

It is a given that however large your house or office is, you could always do with a little extra space, just one more room that would make all the difference. Many architects start their careers by addressing this need, by designing extensions that are either in keeping with the original building or form a deliberate contrast to it.

Extensions, though, are not 'microarchitecture' since they are not stand-alone structures. But take them away from the house and they become different beasts – independent and often more specialized, since one is more likely to make the effort to reach them for a specific purpose.

The most common use for an additional room is as a summerhouse, a place for relaxation and contemplation, although in the most generous examples these may also be used by guests for sleeping. And, with the growth of people working at home, often the shed or the summer room is converted to a home office. There are numerous companies offering off-the-peg home offices, some of them pleasingly contemporary in design. But even this is not an original idea. The British writer George Bernard Shaw, for example, wrote in a converted summerhouse in his garden at Ayot St Lawrence, Hertfordshire, England, through the first half of the twentieth century. Built with castors that fitted onto a circular track, it could rotate to face the sun.

There are other strands of more fanciful thinking, often seen today in conceptual ideas coming out of art colleges, architectural students' work or thought up by young practices. Again these have precedents in, for example, the work of Haus-Rucker-Co, founded in Vienna in 1967. In an era when space travel and technology were as exciting as newly discovered mind-expanding drugs, this practice, set up by Laurids Ortner, Günter Zamp Kelp and Klaus Pinter, came up with ideas such as the Balloon for Two. Suspended outside the architects' office, this allowed them to sit outside and enjoy a new experience.

Another Haus-Rucker-Co project, and one that was entirely independent of a building, was the Yellow Heart, which consisted of a pulsating bubble inside an inflatable capsule. Inside, two people could relax in a bed while enjoying the inflation/deflation rhythm of the air that was pumped in sequence into the chamber. Now people seeking that kind of other-worldly experience are more likely to choose tree houses, such as the delightful Free Spirit Spheres designed by Tom Chudleigh (see page 204). Similar in feeling are the O_2

Sustainability Tree Houses, designed by Dustin Feider. Based on Buckminster Fuller domes, these are lightweight structures, slung between trees.

While Minneapolis-based Feider sees his tree houses as places for contemplation, Australian architect Andrew Maynard has a more serious purpose with his proposal for a Global Rescue Station Generation 2. This is to help with the campaign to prevent clear felling of the previously untouched Styx Valley Forest in western Tasmania. Protesters have already created Generation 1 by putting a structure into one of the oldest trees. Maynard's proposal is for a little wooden building that would be attached not to one but to three trees by metal collars. Tall and nar-row, it would consist of two rooms stacked above each other, the lower containing an office and lavatory, and the upper for sleeping in.

Building extra space in the garden or even the nearby woods is a great idea as long as you have either owner-ship or access, but if you are stuck in an apartment you may still feel the need for more room without having the land to build on. Don't despair – ingenious proposals exist even for these conditions. One is from Dutch practice Hof-man Dujardin Architecten, which has come up with a concept called Bloomframe. Intended for people without balconies, it aims to offer them some outdoor space with a kind of pivoting window frame that folds out to create a balcony and then can be stowed away again. This will not be for sufferers from vertigo, as it has a glass floor, but it does not require as much courage as a proposal from Berlin-based company Realities: United. This is a pivoting seat that swings out to allow you to be suspended above the city, enjoying fresh air and even the view, if you have the courage to look. Because it is mounted internally and only swings out on a tempo-rary basis, it would, says the

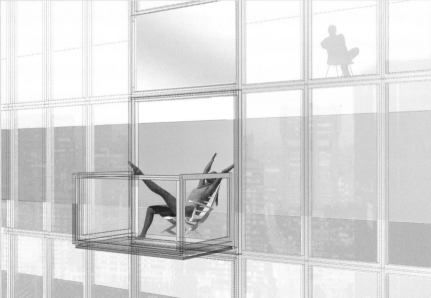

Below left: Hotel Everland,
Switzerland, Sabina Lang
and Daniel Baumann, 2002.
The portable hotel suite can
be craned into any desired
location, including rooftops.

Below right: The sleek interior of an Everland suite.

company, not be subject to
any planning constraints.
One can, however, foresee
other objections.

If you have no ground, and
are not brave enough to
hang out of the window,
another place to put a new
structure is on the roof.
There are structures such
as Werner Aisslinger's Loft-
cube, a complete apartment
that can be craned onto a
roof, or more conceptual
work such as ex.studio's
Point of View lookout in
Tuscany (see page 208).

Somewhere between the
two is Everland, a project
by Swiss artists Sabina Lang
and Daniel Baumann,
which is a single port-
able hotel suite in a bright
green-and-white enclosure.
Making its debut at Yverdon
on Lake Neuchâtel as part
of the Swiss Expo in 2002,
it later spent 15 months
from the middle of 2006
on the roof of the Museum
of Modern Art in Leipzig,
Germany, before moving on
to Paris and then Tokyo.

EMERSON SAUNA

Movement in architecture is always engaging, and with the sauna building he has designed for a house in Duluth, Minnesota, architect David Salmela of Salmela Architect has created an illusion of movement that sets up a delightful visual tension. It looks as if the building's pitched roof has nearly slid off lengthways, and is now propped on a circular brick column. Although you know it is not going to happen, you wait to see if it is going to slide back again. But this is not just a witty one-liner. Salmela exhibits a grasp of geometry and a usage of materials that has won several prizes for the building. Indeed, the judges of the AIA Minnesota Honor Award called it 'a gorgeous little poem of a building', and this does not seem like hyperbole.

Salmela designed the building in the verdant grounds of a house by Cooke Lake, Duluth. He had designed the main house for Peter and Cynthia Emerson in 1997. Also an award winner, the main house was intended to relate to the vernacular forms of northern Minnesota, but with the sauna building Salmela settled for pure geometry and some reassuringly solid materials.

Part of what makes the building so satisfactory is that Salmela has thought hard about the different functions it embraces. What do you want with a sauna? You want to get very hot, you want to cool down, either indoors or outside, and at some point you want a shower. Salmela has combined these functions in a manner that is so clever that, while admiring his ingenuity, you feel that it was somehow inevitable.

An inscrutable brick box, with small square windows, contains the sauna and changing rooms. A brick chimney rises from the dead centre of this box, above a grassed flat roof. From the south end of the sauna, you can either walk outside to take an outdoor shower within the supporting brick 'column' – which turns out to only be a semicircle – or go upstairs into the space beneath the pitched gable roof. This roof, clad in thin strips of timber, covers the 'cooling porch', a space that is glazed at the south end and open to the grass roof at the north end. The simple beds and benches in the cooling porch are arranged with a geometric rigour that reflects the rest of the design.

The stark geometry imposed throughout this little structure, in total only 3.7 metres x 7.4 metres (12 feet x 24 feet), could feel overly constraining in a building that was meant to be used in a variety of ways. But here, where there is total dedication only to the sauna and its rituals, it is not only appropriate but also adds to the pleasure that the owners must feel in such restrained luxury.

Below: The uncompromising nature of the sauna building contrasts with the house's nod to Minnesota vernacular architecture.

Bottom: A column supporting the pitched-roof structure also houses the outdoor shower.

Overleaf: The sauna room with (behind the chimney) the semi-open cooling porch.

Below left: A grass roof
surrounding the chimney
is accessible from the cooling porch.

Below right: Section, upper-
level and lower-level plans.

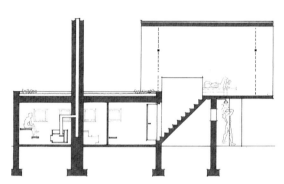

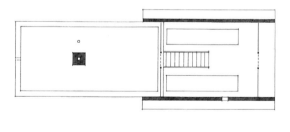

Below left: Simple furnish-
ings and ubiquitous timber
make the cooling porch a
place of repose.

Below right: Brick is ex-
posed on the inside of the
sauna room.

SAUNA BOX

Do you fancy the idea of a sauna, but your choice of location is a bit inaccessible, or you may even wish to move the sauna around a bit? Then Toronto, Canada-based Castor Canadensis has the answer for you: the 1,500-kilo (3,300-pound) Sauna Box, made from the 2.4-metre (8-foot) chopped-off end of a shipping container. The three designers who make up the Castor Canadensis co-operative are a metalsmith, a stone carver and a graphic designer. In a mild attempt to shock, they declare on their website: 'Contact us if you want good-looking shit for your home or your project.' On offer at present is anything from heavy but elegant furniture to tee-shirts and knitted hats.

The decision to use an old shipping container was not an economic one but was taken for reasons of durability and love of the look. 'I started to build a wood-framed sauna at my farm,' Brian Boucher (the stone carver), told Toronto's *Globe and Mail*, 'But it didn't make sense. The shipping container is just a way cooler aesthetic – and it'll last about 10,000 years.' At Can $20,000 (US $18,000), the retail price is no less than for a more traditional solution, so it is not aimed at bargain hunters. The trio cheekily claim that their target customer is that most architecturally aware of film stars, Brad Pitt.

With an outer skin of Corten steel, the weathering steel that grows its own protective layer of rust, the Sauna Box is certainly tough, with an aesthetic to match. Internally, it is gentler, with cedar panelling and a cedar bench, a custom-made wood-burning stove, and a stool carved by the cooperative from a single block of limestone. Round in section, it tapers at the centre in a manner the trio describe as 'beaver gnawed' – after all Castor Canadensis is the American beaver. With solar panels to generate the electricity to power the lights, the Sauna Box can be totally self-sufficient, and also secure when it is locked up tight. Optional extras include a special iPod to play sauna-type music, and a showerhead that can easily be rigged just outside the box itself – although evidently this will require a water supply.

Many of those working with adapting shipping containers for architectural purposes are intrigued by the idea of mass production, but this is not part of Castor Canadensis' approach. The members warn that, 'The beaver is only going to produce a limited number – so if you want to get hot in the box, give us a call.' If Brad Pitt does decide that this is what he needs, he won't have to worry about all the neighbours having one as well.

Below left: Have sauna, will travel.

Below right: Inside the aesthetic is gentler, with cedar panelling and a 'beaver gnawed' stool.

Bottom: Designed to be entirely self-sufficient, the sauna is at home in a remote setting.

SUMMERHOUSE

Using mirrors to create an illusion of space is an old trick but one that is repeated frequently because it is so successful. It works inside buildings and also in gardens, sometimes as a way of brightening a dark corner, and sometimes to enlarge the dimensions.

Young architects Sylvia Ullmayer and David Sylvester have taken this concept further with their garden pavilion in north London by putting a mirrored finish on one wall. This works because the illusion is not dependent on deception. One knows exactly what is being done, and yet the eye is still fooled. By doing this, their pavilion does not reduce the garden but seems, from vital angles, actually to make it bigger.

Putting extra space into a garden is also a cliché but it is one that has been addressed here with intelligence, thanks to clients who are as design-aware and precise as the architects. David and Sybil Caines were living in a three-bedroom flat that

they loved, with two sons aged six and ten. They didn't want to move, but they badly needed more space, and they saw building in the garden, which is 61 metres (200 feet) long, as a way of achieving that. David Caines is a graphic designer, and had a sense of what he wanted to achieve although, as Ullmayer said, 'he didn't know anything about materials'. He knew that he loved the simplicity of the Eames houses in California, and also that he wanted the extra space to provide a place where he could paint, family and entertaining space, including somewhere to play table tennis, and a tool shed for his wife's gardening implements.

The architects started with the idea of a simple box shape, but responded to the clients' requirements, the shape of the garden and existing plants by kinking it. This bend in the horizontal plane is echoed in the vertical plane, by a butterfly roof of polycarbonate that drains to the centre.

Although supported on a steel structure on concrete pad foundations, the building's principal material is plywood. The walls were constructed so beautifully that the architects decided to plane them off and leave them exposed, the internal ribs providing a rectilinear structure that can act as shallow shelves. Along with the knots in the timber, and the ends of the screw holes, they add a level of visual interest.

The mirror finish on the 8-metre-long (26-foot-long) side wall is a deliberate contrast to these natural materials, but by the very artificiality of its reflectiveness, adds to the feeling of being in the middle of nature, or at least the artificial and splendid interpretation of nature that is an urban garden. Architectural critic Jay Meyrick has written that the summerhouse, 'shimmers playfully in the mind's eye like a cold, crisply cleansing slab of architectural sorbet'. It is certainly a refreshing alternative to the pastiche conservatory or the forbidding garden shed.

Below: The mirrored wall, kinked in the centre, seems to add to the size of the garden and the luxuriance of the planting.

Opposite top: Section through the summerhouse, which sits on simple concrete pad foundations.

Opposite centre: Site plan, showing the direct axis from the house to the pavilion at the end of the garden (right).

Opposite bottom: The polycarbonate roof brings more light into the summerhouse, which has plywood exposed on the inside.

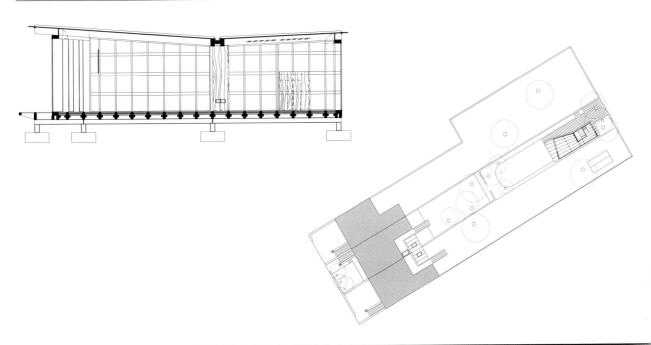

WILLIAM DICKSON
LONDON, UK

JAPANESE GARDEN PAVILION

The complementary formal relationship of interior and exterior space embodied in Japanese garden design is the key influence exploited by architect William Dickson in the remodelling of his own flat's north-facing garden. Within it, the intriguing and deceptively simple pavilion illustrated here occupies one of a number of linked garden 'rooms', which complement and interact with the flat's living spaces, all year round.

The central circulation axis of the flat is extended into the garden, forming a spine along which simple elements are placed: a formal pond, the pavilion, differing planting beds, a Japanese stone and water garden. The garden design achieves great variety with a satisfying economy of means, including its simple geometry and changes of level; vertical and horizontal screening using traditional knotted bamboo fences and cedar slats; and the reflective qualities of water and glass.

The overarching branches of well-established trees and the garden's high walls make this a secret place in which the pavilion acts as vantage point, hide-away, and somewhere to work, eat and entertain. As with any garden, the setting changes through the seasons. Lighting has been integrated within the garden to add another aesthetic dimension at night.

Travel in Japan and Scandinavia influenced the construction details, and this is to be seen in the refined, elemental way the design of pavilion, stone pond, deck and fences is handled.

Shaded by the canopy of branches, the pavilion is composed of two elements: a simple glazed room, and an outer enclosure formed by slatted roof and wall screens.

The basic glass box, small enough to feel like a study for one person but big enough for four to dine under the stars, is framed in black-stained pine. There are two glass doors in opposite corners and a patent-glazed roof on a minimal slope. German smoked oak flooring sits on a damp-proof layer, which in turn sits on top of a Norwegian pine deck supported on pine posts and foundations. The black-stained pine outer frame supports a brise-soleil roof and side screens, both clad in 3 x 6-centimetre (1 x 2-inch) western red cedar slats.

This, however, forms only one element of the shading strategy. There are blinds inside the box, and poles for hanging curtains. In addition, the intermeshed branches of two trees – a whitebeam and a tree of heaven – provide cool shade in the summer.

The surrounding bamboo fences are of the misugaki pattern, knotted in black twine. In front of the pavilion is a shallow square pool lined in limestone, which provides great reflections especially in the evening when the lights are on in the pavilion.

As you move round the garden, the warm red of the outer screen and the black of the structure shift in relation to each other, creating constantly changing impressions.

The pavilion fulfils the idea of a place apart within the garden, distinct, yet nicely forming a full stop to the axial view from the house. With background heating and its range of shading options, there is almost no time of year when it cannot be used. Summer visitors occasionally sleep there, perfectly screened from the upstairs neighbours. In turn, the upstairs occupants are protected from intrusive activity and glare from the pavilion's lights. Other elements of this small garden's masterplan are a sauna and a Scottish-style 'sitooterie' in the grotto, the pergola roof of which reflects exactly the scale and design of the pavilion's slatted brise-soleil.

Below: The limestone-
bottomed pool provides
magnificent reflections of
the pavilion.

Opposite: Strips of western red cedar were used for the outer, shading enclosure.

Bottom left: The pavilion was constucted around an existing tree.

Below: The pavilion was designed to provide pleasure at all times of the year, not just in summer.

Bottom right: Dickson is transforming the whole garden, using traditional Japanese techniques for the fencing.

BUTTERFLY PORCH

The lightweight 'butterfly roof' that is the crowning glory of this well-considered house extension has to carry a substantial weight of expectation and acclaim. Architect Rick Harlan Schneider was selected by Forbes.com in 2006 as one of its ten 'Tastemakers Architecture'. It placed him against such international names as Santiago Calatrava, Frank Gehry, Zaha Hadid and Renzo Piano, admitting that he is 'hardly known outside the Washington, D.C., area', but arguing that 'Schneider is turning heads locally with his use of green architecture. His lofty goal is to reposition the architecture profession toward a more ethical environmental view.' To which the instinctive response is, 'So what?' Those aspirations are becoming increasingly common, and many who embrace them are also good architects.

But if Forbes seems to have over-lauded Schneider, this does not negate the fact that the practice has an impressive portfolio of work. The Butterfly Porch is an elegant small building that responded both to the client's requirements and to discoveries made on site in the course of construction.

Porches are attractive in places with warm humid summers, where there may be summer rain and a need for screens to keep out the bugs, but where one wants to benefit from every available breeze. Bethesda, Maryland, where the Butterfly Porch was built, has conditions that are pretty average for the US and fits this profile well. In July, the hottest month, average daily highs are just below 32°C (90°F), and at night temperatures only drop to about 18°C (65°F). Rainfall for the month is about 10 centimetres (4 inches).

Elisa Rappaport, the client, wanted to recreate childhood memories of meals eaten outside to the accompaniment of the sound of crickets. When Inscape Studio started to look at her existing house and her requirements, however, it came up with a solution quite different from most porches.

Traditionally a porch forms part of the main structure of the house, but here it is a separate room with a linking bridge that acts as an external deck. There were several reasons for this. Rappaport wanted her porch near to the kitchen, but Schneider was concerned not to cut off all light to that room. Also, since Rappaport did not necessarily want the porch built in a manner in keeping with her colonial-style house, it was easier to give the imagination a free rein if the new structure was clearly separate.

The final position and orientation were chosen with the garden and views very much in mind, and with a concern for the environment in both the siting of foundations and the materials used. It is built from softwood that has been pressure-treated with non-toxic chemicals and uses cedar cladding from trees that have been harvested sustainably. The cladding was carefully positioned to frame the best views, and has large enough gaps between the boards to allow the breezes in – the effect is of enclosure rather than containment. Tube footings support both the building itself and, separately, the roof. They have a small area to minimize damage to the ground, and the initial positions were changed once the presence of a shallow tree root was discovered. The contractor took great care to counteract the effect of compaction caused by construction workers treading on the ground repeatedly.

The butterfly roof, supported on a lightweight metal structure, had to be lifted in by crane. It serves a dual purpose – both giving an enormous visual lift to the porch, and collecting rainwater that is channelled down a hanging chain to a rainwater butt. This will be used to irrigate a planned 'rain garden' that in turn will reduce run-off from the house and garden – part of the overall environmental strategy that impressed Forbes so much. It doesn't seem bad to me either.

Below left: Deck plan showing how the porch relates
to the house while remaining structurally and visually
independent of it.

Below right: Diagram
showing the build-up of the
porch, with the roof and its
supports structurally independent of the enclosure.

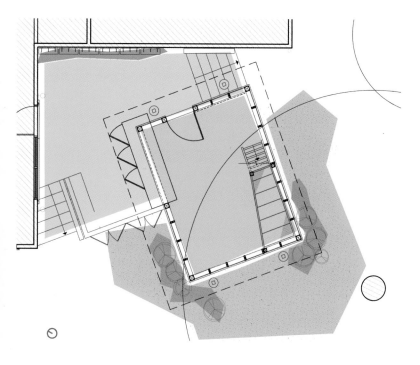

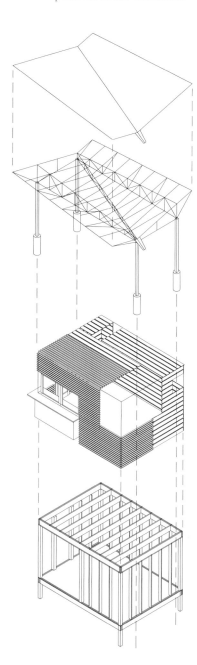

Below left: Cedar cladding is
sufficiently widely spaced to
allow breezes to penetrate.

Below right: The asym-
metric butterfly roof gives
presence to the pavilion and
relates more closely to the
scale of the house.

GARDEN HUT

Instinct might tell you that the last material you wanted to plonk down in a charmingly rural Spanish setting would be a load of rusty metal. But instinct, as so often, would be wrong.

That is demonstrated by this exquisitely crafted little structure, designed by two UK-based architects, that sits in a generous garden in the wheat-growing country near Girona, northeast Spain. Because of the rolling nature of the countryside, the hut, as it is modestly described, is visible from quite some distance. Visible, that is, if you look for it carefully, because it is has a disconcerting tendency to blend in to its surroundings.

The architects, British-born Rita Lambert and Artur Carulla, who did his initial training in Barcelona, say that they chose to use Corten steel because it echoes the colour of the local roof tiles. More properly known as 'weathering steel', Cor-ten has its own very important patina. It starts rusting from the moment it is exposed to the air, but this rust forms an airproof layer that prevents the metal underneath being attacked. With time it turns first a bright orange colour, then eventually a dark, purplish brown. Certainly in its orangey state it blends remarkably well with the surroundings, particularly when the wheat is ripening at the end of the summer.

Indeed, from a distance the most dominant elements are likely to be the two triangular laminated glass skylights, if the sun is angled so that it reflects off them. The fact that the skylights are triangular is an indication that the hut is not straightforward in terms of geometry, despite having a rectangular plan. It has a multi-pitched roof, an unconventional approach that one might expect once one knows that both architects previously worked for Peter Eisenman. And the building is also designed to serve two very different functions – as a closed-up store in the damp winter months, and as an outdoor room in the summer. It can therefore open up to reveal an interior of durable Brazilian ipe timber, used not only as a lining but also for cabinets and the surround to a sink.

The intention, say the architects, was that the hut should act as part of the house, but it is such an intriguing object in its own right that it has a definite identity of its own. However, they also say that they want it to be 'like a piece of furniture', and that its 'fragmented geometry encourages visitors to walk around it, while it is refusing to reveal its geometry'. This air of mystery makes it an unexpected but delightful adornment to a setting that already has so much to offer.

Below: Spot the building
– hidden on the left-hand
side of the image, the
garden hut's warm colour
blends well with ripe corn
and vernacular buildings.

Below left: The hut in its closed state, and …

Bottom left: … opened up, with one side almost disappearing.

Below right: Plan of the hut showing how the side panels open up.

Bottom right: Durable Brazilian ipe timber has been used for the interior.

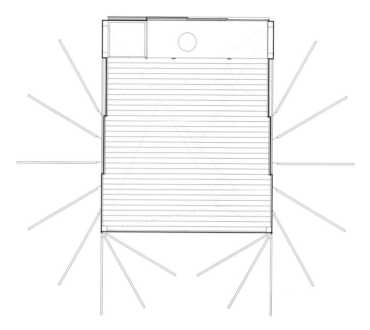

Below: Two triangular
skylights are at angles that
often reflect the sun.

PETER PAN HOUSE

Architects' children may have more fun than others. With home often a building site for years of their childhood, their parents cannot be over-cautious about safety. And if those parents also choose to apply their skills to create imaginative places for play, they may end up with some very superior equipment indeed.

Such at least is the good fortune of the children of London husband and wife team Amir Sanei and Abigail Hopkins. In the back garden of their Suffolk second home, the duo first created a Wendy house for their daughters. They subverted the usual twee domesticity (not to the complete pleasure of their clients, then aged three and four) by using fence posts, recycled windows and corrugated metal sheeting for the roof.

Having some of the corrugated metal, more usually used for Suffolk pig arcs, remaining, they then set about creating a structure for their sons as well. But this was less about creating a home in miniature than about adventurous play.

The curved metal is formed into a tube, slung from trees, that has openings at the sides so that the 'inhabitants' can look out. Given the genesis of the main material, Sanei and Hopkins created a story that this was a house for 'flying pigs', justifying the fact that it is just 2 metres (6 1/2 feet) off the ground with the argument that 'pigs can't fly very high'. But the interior is definitely designed with small humans in mind, with benching running along its length and a step in the middle against which to brace one's feet.

In today's risk-averse culture, Sanei Hopkins' ingenious creations have not received universal acclaim, with doubters arguing that hands could be cut by metal edges and that the entire enterprise is risky and in contravention of health and safety legislation – not to mention being bad for the trees!

But the structure at least appeals strongly to children's sense of adventure. Having created a Wendy house for the girls, it was unsurprising that the architects named its masculine companion Peter Pan, after the eponymous hero of J. M. Barrie's play. Boys fortunate enough to enjoy such a wonderful playhouse may well decide that they never want to grow up.

Below left: Constructed from material used for pig arcs, the structure hangs from trees and appeals to a *Boy's Own* sense of adventure.

Below right: An earlier creation was a Wendy house for the couple's daughters.

Bottom right: Benching and a step make the Peter Pan house comfortable.

SCHLAFHAUS

Marco Koeppel and Carlo Martinez evolved this 'sleep house' in the Asturias region of Spain, having spent a long time considering it as a project. Growing from the concept of a *traumhaus* (dream house), it developed into a Zeppelin shape, perched lightly on the ground as if ready to float away. It borrows both from the local tradition of the *hórreo* (granary), a structure raised up on legs to protect it from damp and vermin, and from the 1960s Finnish ellipsoid Futuro house designed by Matti Suuronen.

However, in terms of materials, the Schlafhaus is very different from either of its precursors, turning its back both on the stone solidity of the *hórreo* and on the fibreglass and plastics employed on Futuro. Instead it sits on steel legs, with the main body built from timber and stretched canvas, materials much closer to those used in the Zeppelin that it so closely resembles. The curved wooden ribs were cut using a CNC (computer numerically controlled) wood plotter, which was very new technology in 1998 when this project began. It made achieving the curves relatively simple and inexpensive, whereas previously it would have involved a lot of costly work by skilled carpenters.

In contrast, when the designers looked at futuristic fabrics for the covering, inspecting, for example, a variant of Gore-Tex, they ended up concluding that nothing would serve as well as the waxed cotton that they had used on an earlier project. So waxed cotton it was.

In the manner of self-build projects, it took about four years from construction of the main frame to completion of the whole building in 2002.

Internally, the plan circulates around the oval form, as dictated by the fact that the access stairs come into the centre of the structure. There are both conventional windows and skylights, and the structure is large enough to include a bed built onto a timber platform, a full-size bath, and cupboards for storage. The bed is in a cocoon-like enclosure, the ribs are exposed elegantly on the interior, and it is possible to lie in bed and look at the stars. This is an ideal *traumhaus*.

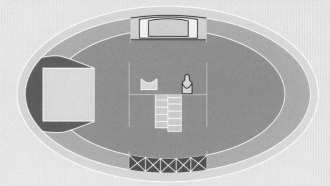

Opposite: Plan of the
structure.

Below: Dream or nightmare?
The finished building looks
like a shiny spaceship.

Bottom, left to right: Structural model, and the *traumhaus* under construction.

DOGTROT

Betsy and Shane Williamson's practice in Toronto, founded in 2002, likes to pursue theoretical projects as well as commissions. The Dogtrot house is a bit of both – an idea that the duo has developed, but also a response to a commission from a real client.

It marries two ideas – the acceptability of the out-building as a typology in southern Ontario where, if the area is 9 square metres (100 square feet) or less no planning permission is needed, and the southwestern United States' historic concept of the dogtrot house.

Why dogtrot? Because this house type consisted of two cabins linked by an open porch, through which a dog could, of course, trot but where, in fact, it was more likely to lie, enjoying the breeze that was much of the rationale for the design. This was plantation architecture and, cramped and dark as the original may appear to modern eyes, the dogtrot was actually several levels above the meanest form of housing. Typically self-built

of timber, most houses were very dark inside. In the humid heat of states such as Louisiana, the greatest concerns were staying dry and, in the summer, keeping cool.

The simplest form of house was a straightforward 'pen', probably just one room, perhaps with a kitchen attached. The dogtrot was far more aspirational, consisting of two pens (the second probably built later), typically unified by a long veranda and with external chimneys at one or both ends. The dogtrot itself, the space between the two units, was typically half the width of a single pen, about 2.4 metres (8 feet) wide. By funnelling any breeze through, it offered a primitive form of air conditioning and also brought in some much needed light, since these houses typically had shutters rather than window glass.

The climatic conditions of southern Ontario are rather different, and indeed these outbuildings are considered very much as single-season

dwellings, since they are not insulated against the winter cold. With summers relatively short but warm, there is a desire to spend as much time as possible out of doors.

This is the yearning for which the Williamsons have catered, cleverly getting past the planning constraints by creating two separate adjacent structures, each of less than 9 square metres (100 square feet). These can be used for storage during the winter and are shut up securely against, as one commentator put it, 'marauding snowmobiles'. Then in summer the internal walls come down, and instead of being a mere passageway the dogtrot becomes a place in which one can sit and admire the beauty outside.

The level of affluence and indulgence enjoyed by the Williamsons' clients is way above that of the plantation dwellers who first invented the dogtrot, but if the latter were around today they might well recognize and admire the level of ingenuity, and the creation of

as much amenity as possible from limited resources.

Bottom left: The dogtrot
in two proposed configu-
rations.

Below left: In summer, the
house would open up with a
passage through it offering
light, ventilation and views.

Below right: Floor plan,
complete with typical views.

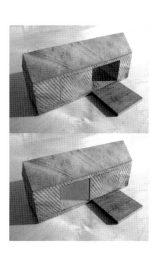

TOM CHUDLEIGH
BRITISH COLUMBIA, CANADA

FREE SPIRIT SPHERES

A few years ago on the roads of British Columbia, you might have seen a pick-up truck towing the most extraordinary timber bubble. Rather like a wooden eyeball, it looked both playful and intriguing as well as appearing to want to roll off and escape. What was it and where would it go?

It was Eryn, the second and larger of two 'free spirit spheres' designed and made by Tom Chudleigh, the precursors of what he hopes will be a number of off-the-shelf solutions.

Just looking at this ball trying to escape the restrictions of the road makes you smile, and the idea of inhabiting one of these spheres is immensely appealing. Chudleigh has thought through every detail carefully, and has come up with a solution that not only does not damage the trees, but will also keep the occupants safe even if a branch comes crashing down. What could be nicer than to climb a spiral stair with a tree trunk at its centre, cross a tiny drawbridge and go into

the sphere, through whose portholes you can look out at the forest canopy or up at the stars? The sphere will sway gently in the breeze or, because of its lightness and low centre of gravity, respond more vigorously when somebody moves inside it.

British Columbia boasts that few places on earth can match the richness and diversity of its forest lands, so where better to start a business supplying these suspended homes? The spheres can be hung as high as the trees will permit, so on the west coast of Canada they could go up to 35 metres (115 feet) in the old-growth Douglas firs, although Chudleigh does admit that 'this gets a little scary' – not to mention involving a long walk up. Eryn is 3.2 metres (10 1/2 feet) in diameter and made from Sitka spruce, whereas Eve, the smaller prototype, is only 2.8 metres (9 feet) across and made from yellow cedar. In both cases, the sphere is built up from two layers of laminated timber, with the outer surface

sanded and then covered with two layers of woven fibreglass roving set in epoxy. The spheres are insulated, and vinyl upholstery fabric is stapled to the inner surface along the 'lines of longitude', with the joints covered in timber strip. Fixing is by three cables to three different trees, giving considerable stability with enough redundancy that, were one bough to break this baby would not fall.

Internally, there is a relatively small flat floor area, but Chudleigh has fitted out Eryn with comforts including a double bed and considerable storage space. Its rather folksy fittings contrast with the dramatic views of tree tops through porthole windows that follow the curvature of the sphere. The timber door, which opens outwards like the hatchway to a submarine, also forms part of the sphere.

Chudleigh's design includes power cabling so that heating and lighting are included, but with no water supply or waste extract, the 'house' cannot include a bathroom.

His ambition, however, is to create a colony of around ten spheres, with a self-contained sewage plant below.

His inclination is clearly towards a kind of semi-mystical contemplative use, but even if that does not appeal there is a great attraction in the idea of spending the night in one of Chudleigh's gently bobbing spheres among the tree tops – as long as you don't mind clambering down all those stairs to reach the lavatory.

Below left: The spiral stair
winds up around one of
the three trees to which the
sphere is attached.

Below right: Framing of
the sphere.

Left: Portholes offer magnificent views of trees.

Below: Electricity is brought into the sphere.

Bottom left: Careful fitting out allows a surprising level of comfort.

Bottom right: Timber strips cover the joints between the vinyl upholstery.

POINT OF VIEW

The beautiful solidity of old Italian houses is not always conducive to great views. The very charm of the urban planning, even in relatively small places, means that buildings are close together, and windows are often tiny, to provide protection from the summer heat. The medieval town of Casale Marittimo, near the Tuscan coast, is just such a place. Rising high above the former marshland of the Maremma, it is a sickle-shaped gathering of tightly packed buildings, few of which actually offer views of the sea and beyond to Corsica.

The architects Patricia Meneses and Iván Juárez of ex.studio are based in Barcelona, also on the Mediterranean, but perhaps because they are not natives of this coast, coming originally from Mexico, they are particularly sensitive to the importance of such views.

In May 2005 they became involved with an art project called Luogo: Comune in which eight international artists were invited to make interventions in the Italian town, addressing in some way the sense of space. ex.studio made two such interventions.

One was to perch a very lightweight 'observatory' on the top of one of those solid ochre-washed houses. Looking from the ground as if it could blow away in a puff of wind, it was in fact a relatively robust construction of a couple of curved wire members supporting a mesh enclosure. The idea was that from that point one could sit and watch the landscape by day or the stars at night, or just sit and think surrounded by nature and the sky. So great was the incongruity in terms of the context that it became a charming ornament on the roof top.

The second intervention was a little way out of the town, on the gentle summit of a hill. In the middle of a field, the architects created a belvedere from bales of straw. This obviously man-made intervention, although constructed from materials in keeping with its setting, encouraged people to stand and look out, or to sit within it and look at the sky.

Projects such as Luogo: Comune always attract visitors from elsewhere, whose experience of the Tuscan countryside would have been enhanced by these interventions. But even more importantly, those who have lived there all their lives may also have been encouraged to see their environment with fresh eyes.

Below left: Curved wire members form the observatory's enclosure.

Below right: Mesh encloses the viewer but allows views of the countryside.

Bottom: The lightweight observatory is perched on top of a very solid house.

Overleaf: In the architects' second intervention in the area, straw bales formed a belvedere that made familiar views less familiar.

GILLES EBERSOLT
PARIS, FRANCE

SUSPENDED OFFICE

The suspended office that Gilles Ebersolt 'designed' for a photographer friend is an excellent demonstration of the fact that the most important element in architecture is having the idea. In this case, circumstances dictated that Ebersolt produced no more than the concept and a quick sketch, but the result certainly has his stamp on it.

Ebersolt is an architect who has carved an unconventional corner for himself. He specializes in inflatable and suspended structures, whether floating high over forest canopies (see page 90) or as bubbles to be animated from within and used for performance. So when photographer Xavier Lucchesi approached Ebersolt and asked him to tackle the need for extra space in his studio, he must have expected an unconventional solution.

As befits an architect of mobile elements, Ebersolt leads a peripatetic life. Unable immediately to think of anything more imaginative than a simple mezzanine, which would compromise the proportions and light in the studio, Ebersolt set off almost immediately for Morocco. While he was there, he visited a dilapidated grandiose villa and saw, on a terrace, a magnificent if scruffy-looking swing seat. Immediately he thought of this as the solution to Lucchesi's problem, photographed it and, once he got back to France, showed Lucchesi the picture.

The idea appealed, and Ebersolt quickly sketched out the idea in three dimensions and left it with Lucchesi. Then he left for two months in Panama. When he came back, he met Lucchesi in the street, who told him 'the suspended office is complete'. Ebersolt says that he couldn't believe it, 'Normally,' he explains, 'I have to do 36 drawings and all sorts of details, before finally the project is abandoned!' In this case, however, Lucchesi had called on old friends from Marseilles who had technical expertise and relished the new challenge. They built the workspace up from small pieces, since it had to be installed on the fourth floor, and supported it on iron flats. The floor of the space is glazed, to maximize transparency, and uses scavenged Plexiglas panels from decommissioned telephone boxes. Key elements, such as work surfaces, are built into the structure, so that no other furniture is needed.

The major deviation from Ebersolt's concept is that the structure does not swing, since it is fixed to an access stair. However, it achieves its main aim admirably, of providing extra space without compromising the studio's magnificent proportions. Indeed, like a piece of sculpture, this obviously separate element sets off its surroundings and enhances them. Not the kind of architect to be precious about his intellectual property, at least not when dealing with a friend, Ebersolt seems delighted that he has contributed so much to Lucchesi's working environment, and with so little effort.

Opposite: Ebersolt's sketch.

Right: The swing seat in Morocco that provided the inspiration for the project.

Below left: The floor is glazed with Plexiglas to maximize transparency.

Below right: The suspended office enhances the double-height studio.

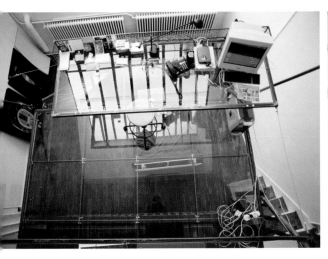

PROJECT CREDITS

A-Z Wagon Stations, California, USA
Concept: Andrea Zittel
Website: www.zittel.org
Illustrated Customizers: Veronica Fernandez and Peter Blackburn (p113);
Hal McFeely (p112 tl); Jennifer Nocon (p112 bl); Andrea Zittel and David
Dodge (p112 r)

Bandstand, De La Warr Pavilion, Bexhill-on-Sea, UK
Architect: Níall McLaughlin Architects
Website: www.niallmclaughlin.com
Project Team: Sandra Coppin, Gus Lewis, Níall McLaughlin, Silke Voskoetter
Client: The De La Warr Pavilion Trust – Jill Theis, Alan Haydon (Director)/
Rother District Council – Tony Leonard
Main Contractor: Westside Design Workshops – Michael Mc Hugh
Structural Engineers: Price & Myers – Phil Hudson, Tim Lucas
Acoustic Engineers: Paul Gilleron Acoustics

Bicycle surveillance hut, Scheveningen, The Netherlands
Architect: FAT
Website: www.fat,co,uk
Project Team: Sean Griffiths, Charles Holland, Sam Jacob, Dimitri Kudin
Client: Stroom/City of The Hague
Main Contractor: Kloosterboer Décor

Billboard Building, Motoazabu, Minato-ku, Tokyo, Japan
Architect: Klein Dytham Architecture
Website: www.klein-dytham.com
Project Team: Astrid Klein, Mark Dytham, Yukinari Hisayama, Hiroto Kubo
Client: RISA PARTNERS INC.
General Contractor: Eiger Sangyo
Structural Engineer: Structured Envviironment – Alan Burden, Megumi
Akimoto, Yukiko Harada
M&E Engineer: EOS setsubi + COMODO – Setubi Keikaku

Bocce Pavilion, Melbourne, Australia
Architect: Di Mase Architects Pty. Ltd
Website: www.dimasearchitects.com.au
Client: City of Yarra – Stuart Grant
Builder: DJO Constructions – Dan Olle
Engineer: Maurice Farrugia + Associates
User Groups: Montemurro Bocce Club and North Carlton Railway Station
Neighbourhood House

Breckenridge Perfect Cottage, USA
Architect: Christopher C. Deam
Website: www.cdeam.com
Project Team: Christopher C. Deam (principal designer), Steven Heugli
(project architect), Tim Howard (Breckenridge owner), Bob Philips (project
manager, Breckenridge).

Client: Builder – Breckenridge
All engineering, consulting, etc. was handled by Breckenridge in-house.

Bus shelters, Bradford, UK
Architect: Bauman Lyons Architects Ltd
Website: www.baumanlyons.co.uk
Structural engineer: Martin Stockley Associates
Artist: Greyworld
Artist: Forced Entertainment
Client: The Culture Company for METRO
Main contractor: Dobson Construction
Specialist steelwork: J. Bentley Fabrications

Butterfly Porch, Bethesda, Maryland, USA
Architect: Inscape Studio
Website: www.InscapeStudio.com
Project Team: Petros Zouzoulas (project architect), Rick Harlan Schneider
(design principal)
Client: Rapaport + Schoenbaum
Main Contractor: DMI

Camping cabins, La Torerera, Calañas, Huelva, Spain
Architect: Ubaldo García Torrente
E-mail address: UBALDOGTORRENTE@telefonica.net
Client: Consejería de Obras Públicas y Transportes, Junta de Andalucia,
Building Contractor: Coinmer S.L.
Technical Supervisor: Juan Luis Yáñez Sempere

Capsule pigeon loft, Caudry, France
Architecture and graphics: Matali Crasset – Matali Crasset Productions
Website: www.matalicrasset.com
Project Team: Oscar Diaz, Marco Salgado, Francis Fichot
Client: Fondation de France as part of the 'Nouveaux Commanditaires'
programme
Production and mediation: artconnexion, Lille
Partners: Fondation de France, Région Nord-Pas de Calais, Union
Européenne (FEDER), Ville de Caudry
Contractor: Francial SA, Base de Loisirs du Val du Riot.

Cardboard House, Sydney, Australia
Architect: Stutchbury and Pape
Website: www.stutchburyandpape.com.au
Project Team: Peter Stutchbury, Richard Smith, Matt Markham-lee, Maria
Aragao, Emma Neville, Federica De Vito, Marika Jarv, Sacha Zehnder, Rachel
Hudson, Genny Castelli
Building Team: Col James, Adriano Pupilli, Eboni James, Hugo Monline,
Mat Lipson, Caroline Comino, Brendon Miller
Client: Ian Buchan Fell Housing Research Unit, University of Sydney
– Col James

Principal Sponsor: Visy Industries – Peter Cunneen, Leon Maree
Site Managers: Multiplex – Alvin Sayareth, Marco Salvati
Engineering: Professor Max Irvine, Dr David Gunaratnam, Barry Young

Concrete Canvas shelter
Designer: Concrete Canvas Technology
www.concretecanvas.co.uk
Project Team: Peter Brewin, Will Crawford
Major Contractor: Walkerpack Ltd. – Technicover Division

Das Park Hotel, Linz, Austria
Architect: Andreas Strauss

Desert Seal
Architect: Architecture and Vision
Website: www.architectureandvision.com
Project Team: Andreas Vogler, Arturo Vittori
Sales Engineer: Valentina Bomisacci
Project Engineer: Mario Cloeta
Chief Project Engineer: Giacomo Giovangrossi
Prototype Engineer: Patrizio Fedeli
Sales Executive: Fabio Piccolo
Support and Collaboration: Roberto Vittori, European Astronauts Corps, Cologne, Germany; Aero Sekur SpA Aprilia (Latina), Italy; VHF-Technologies SA, Yverdon-Les-Bains, Swotzerland; ESA Technology Transfer Office, Noordwjick, The Netherlands; Museum of Modern Art, New York

Dogtrot, Ontario, Canada
Architect: WILLIAMSONWILLIAMSON
Website: www.williamsonwilliamson.com
Project Team: Betsy Williamson, Shane Williamson (principals), Stephen Griffin (assistant)
Client: Private

Emerson Sauna, Duluth, Minnesota, USA
Architect: Salmela Architect
Website: www.Salmelaarchitect.com
Project Team: David Salmela (principal), Souliyahn Keoboungpheng, Tia Salmela Keobounpheng
Client: Peter and Cynthia Emerson
General Contractor: Rod & Sons Carpentry
Landscape Architect: Coen + Partners
Engineer: Carroll Franck & Associates
Masonry Contractor: Johnston Masonry
Wood Windows: Loewen
Hardware: Rocky Mountain
Downlights: Halo
Speciality Lighting: Lucifer
Plumbing: Duravit

Fish Camp, USA
Architect: Rocio Romero
Website: www.rocioromero.com
Client: Cale Bradford & Rocio Romero
Main Contractor: Rocio Romero

Forest Refuge, Spain
Architect: ex.studio

Website: www.ex-studio.net
Project Team: Iván Juárez, Patricia Meneses
Collaborator: Mareike Richter

Free Spirit Spheres, British Columbia, Canada
Designer: Tom Chudleigh (engineer)
Website: www.freespiritspheres.com
Client and Main Contractor: Free Spirit Spheres
Windows: made by Sunburst Skylights from mould designed by Chudleigh

Garden hut, Sant Miquel de Cruilles, Spain
Architect: Eightyseven
Website: www.eightyseven.net
Project Team: Artur Carulla, Rita Lambert
Local Tradesmen

HDW Info Pavilion, Helsinki, Finland
Architect: Helsinki University of Technology: arkkitehtuuri.tkk.fi
Website: www.puu-studio.com
Project Team: Antti Lehto, Teemu Seppänen (concept and design); Uula Kohonen (detail and construction specialist); Markus Wikar (programming); Hannu Hirsi, Lauri Salokangas (structural engineering); Antti Autio, Anna Bevz, Terhi Keski-Vinkka, Sini Meskanen, Aleksi Niemeläinen, Anita Nummi, Eero Puurunen, Ilkka Salminen, Elina Voipio, Jussi Ziegler (Wood-Glass Studio team); prof. Antti-Matti Siikala, Pekka Heikkinen, Risto Huttunen, Pekka Pakkanen (teachers)
Client: Helsinki University of Technology, Department of Architecture
Plywood Components: UPM
Glass: Tamglass, Pilkington
Cnc Milling: Viisax Oy
Lighting: Ensto
Acrylic Glue Tape: 3M
Sponsors: Wood Focus Oy, Tekniska Föreningen I Finland

Katrina Cottage, New Orleans, USA
Architect: Marianne Cusato
Website: www.cusatocottages.com
Project Team: Marianne Cusato, Deborah Slaunwhite
Client: Katrin Cottage 1 – Mississippi Governors Commission for Recovery and Renewal; KC 544 – Lowe's
Main Contractor: Katrina Cottage 1 – Jason Spellings; KC 544 – Andrew Mills and Micah Lewis
Contractors: KC544 – Lowe's; Dietrich Industries (meal framing). KC 1 and LC 544: Hames Hardie Nuilding Products (cement board siding)

Japanese garden pavilion, London, UK
Architect: William Dickson
e-mail address: williamgr.dickson@virgin.net
Project Team: William Dickson, Mayy Baxter (Tsutaya), Mary Greenhalgh (John Cullen Lighting)
Client: William and Anne Dickson
Main Contractor: Tsutaya
Electrical Contractor: Richard Bell

Lilja Meditative Chapel, Oulu, Finland
Architect: Vesa Oiva Arkkitehti SAFA
Website: www.aoa.fi
Client: UPM-Kymmene/UPM Wisa

Main Contractor: Tarmo-Rakenne Oy
Project Guidance: The Wood Studio, Department of Architecture of the University of Oulu
Structural Design: Insinööritoimisto Pekka Heikkilä Oy
Electrical Design: Insinööritoimisto Ylitalo Oy
Manufacture of Wooden Units: Suomen Rakennustuote Oy

Lookout Tower, Korkeasaari Zoo, Helsinki, Finland
Architectural Design: HUT (The Helsinki University of Technology) Wood Studio/Ville Hara, architect SAFA
Website: www.avan.to
Developer: PWD (Helsinki City Public Works Department) Construction Management
Structural Engineer: DI Hanni Hirsi, DI Lauri Salokangas/Nuovo Engineering

Meditation Dome, Haarlemmermeer, The Netherlands
Architect: Jord den Hollander
e-mail: jdenh@xs4all.nl
Client: Stichting Stiltecentrum, RK dekenaat en SOW kerken
Constructor: Looman & Dupree
Consultant: Arjan Habraken

Micro-compact home (m-ch), Munich, Germany
Architect: Horden Cherry Lee with Haack + Höpfner. The micro compact home design is the copyright of Richard Horden. All rights reserved
Website: c/o Claire Curtis art & architecture publicist. www.clairecurtis.co.uk
Development: Technical University Munich, Professor Richard Horden and his team of assistants and students
Client: Studentenwerk Munich e V commissioned the development and realisation of the O₂ sponsored m-ch village
Main Contractor: m-ch micro compact home production GmbH, Uttendorf
Structural Engineering: Tim Brengelmann, Munich

Microdwellings, Denmark
All credits: N55
Website: www.N55.dk

Miele Space Station, Utrecht, The Netherlands
Architect: 2012 Architecten
Website: www.2012architecten.nl
Project Team: Césare Peeren, Denis Oudendijk
Building Team: Jan Korbes, Jan Jongert, Bart Steenweg, Gijs de Groot, Amanda, Friso Leeflang, Joris Rockx, Steven Barich, Meus Weemhoff, Freya van Dien, Roeland Vergouwen, Aldo Plomp
Client: Cbk Rotterdam/beyond Utrecht
Main Contractor: 2012 Building Team

Ocean Park Hatch Shell, Santa Monica, California, USA
Architect: Tighe Architecture
Website: www.tighearchitecture.com
Project Team: Patrick Tighe, Andy Cao, Yosuke Hoshina, Risa Tsutsumi, Flirian Metz
Client: City of Santa Monica, California
Main Contractor: Tom Farrage & Co.
Landscape Architecture: Andy Cao Landscape

Patjarr Visitor Centre, Western Australia
Name of Student Architects: Oliver Scholz & Niko Young
Website: www.unisa.edu.au/architecture/visitors/projects/patjarr.asp
Project Team: David Morris, Nick Opie, Oliver Scholz, Dr. Michael Tawa
Client: Patjarr Aboriginal Community
Main Contractor: Louis Laybourne Smith School of Architecture & Design, University of South Australia; School of Built Environment, University of New South Wales
Consultant: Dare Sutton Clarke (Engineer)

Peter Pan House, Suffolk, UK
Designer: Sanei Hopkins Architects – Amir Sanei
Website: www.saneihopkins.co.uk

Point of View, Casale Marittimo, Italy
Author: ex.studio
Website: www.ex-studio.net
Architects: Iván Juárez + Patricia Meneses
Promotor: Kforumvienna
Curator: Emmanuele Guidi

pPod Mobile Theatre, Manchester, UK
Architect: magma architecture
Website: www.magmaarchitecture.com
Client: The Horse + Bamboo Centre
Engineers: Buro Happold
Tent Manufacturer: LANCO – Dr. Lange GmbH & Co. KG
Floor Manufacturer: Thein & Rios GmbH
Sponsors: Arts Council England

Projects for the Homeless: Future Shack, Park Bench House and Bus Shelter House, Australia
Architect: Sean Godsell Architecture.
Website: www.seangodsell.com

Public Toilet, Dubrovnik, Croatia
Architect: Nenad Fabijanić
e-mail address: nenad.fabijanic@architekt.hr
Project Team: Sonja Tadej, Maja Nevžala, Snježana Huzanić
Client: City of Dubrovnik
Structural Designer: Božo Ursić
Building Contractor: Gradevinar – Quelin (architect Marko Vetma)

Pushbutton House, USA
Architect: Adam Kalkin
Website: www.architectureandhygiene.com
Project Team: Adam Kalkin, Bem Nollman, Andy Johnston, Matt Nagle, Annan Mozeika, Mikaela Carucci, Dan Garber, Randy Metz, Harry Heissmann, Keiko Mano, Roger Moore
Client: Art Basel/Miami, Deitch Projects
Main Contractor: self-contracted (Quik Build LLC)

Rooftecture S, Kobe, Japan
Architect: Shuhei Endo Architect Institute
Website: www.paramodern.com
Project Team: Shuhei Endo (principal-in-charge), Atsuo Miyatake

Clients: Ryosuke and Yasuko Uenishi
Consultants: Masahashi Ouji, Design-Structure Laboratory

Rotating wind shelters, Blackpool, UK
Architect: Ian McChesney
Website: www.mcchesney.co.uk
Client: Blackpool Borough Council Technical Services
Main Contractor: M-tec (A devision of the WEC Group)
Consultants: Atelier One

Rotorhaus, Germany
Architect: Luigi Colani and Hanse Hause (architect Anette Müller)
Website: www.hanse-haus.de
Client: House used as an exhibition house by Hanse Haus
Main Contractor: Hanse Haus

Sauna Box, Canada
Architect: Castor Canadensis
Website: www.castordesign.ca
Project Team: Brian Richer, Ryan Taylor
Wood Stove: Fenno Manufacturing Ltd.

S(ch)austall, Pfalz, Germany
Architect: FNP Architekten
Website: www.fnp-architekten.de
Project Team: Stefanie Naumann, Martin Naumann
Client: Dr. Marion von Gienanth
Main Contractor: Schulz Zimmerei

Schlafhaus, Asturias, Spain
Architect: Carlosmartinez Architekten
Website: www.carlosmartinez.ch
Project Team: Carlos Martinez, Marco Köppel, Markus Lassan
Client: CALC Artists Navia/España
Main Contractor: Kaufmann Holzbauwerk, Bezau/Austria
Engineer: Merz & Kaufmann, Dornbirn, Austria

SolVin Pretzel, Madagascar
Architect: Gilles Ebersolt assisted by Denis Pegaz Blanc
Website: www.gillesebersolt.com
Client: SolVin and Océan vert
Illustrated: The Madagascar Exploration Project

Spacebox, The Netherlands
Designer: Mart de Jong, Design office De Vijf
Website: www.devijf.com or www.spacebox.info
Manufacturer: Holland Composites Ind
Clients: Delft, Units 123 – DUWO; Utrecht, Units 234 – SSH Utrecht;
Eindhoven, Units 84 – Woningstichting Hertog Hendrik van Lotharingen;
Vlodrop, Units 225 – Maharishi European Research University; Amersfoort,
Units 132 – SCW/Portaal; Hilversum, Units 48 - Patio

Summer Container, Finland
Architect: MH Cooperative
Wensite: www.a-mh.fi
Project Team: Markku Hedman

Client: Suomen Asuntomessut/Finnish Housing Fair Co-operative
Organization
Main Contractor: Schauman Wood Oy

Summerhouse, London, UK
Architect: Ullmayer + Sylvester Architects Ltd.
Website: www.ullmayersylvester.com
Project Team: Allan Sulvester, Silvia Ullmayer
Client: The Caines Family
Main Contractor: TCA and Riverside Construction
Structure: Birdwood Trembath Associates Structural Design (BTA)

Suspended office, Paris, France
Architect: Gilles Ebersolt
Website: www.gillesebersolt.com
Project Team: Gilles Ebersolt, Périne
Name of Client: Xavier Luchesi
Main Contractor: Sud Side

Thermalwing, Mojave Desert, California, USA
Designers: Thermalwing
Website: www.thermalwing.co.uk
Project Team: Tom Ebdon, Lee Halligan, Peter Grove
Client: Ecoshack: organisers of the Greentent Competition
Client contact: Stephanie Smith

Toilet block, Richmond, Tasmania, Australia
Architect: 1+2 Architecture Pty. Ltd
Website: www.1plus2architecture.com
Project Team: Fred Ward, Mike Verdouw, Cath Hall, Piers Chamberlain,
Mark Kukola
Client: Clarence City Council
Master-panning team and Landscape Architecture: 1+2 in collaboration with
Lesley Gulson Landscape Architect
Structural Engineer: Gandy and Roberts Pty. Ltd
Hydraulic Service Engineer: Gandy and Roberts Pty. Ltd
Electrical Service Engineer: SEMF Pty. Ltd
Quantity Surveyor: WT Partnership
Builder: Cordwell Lane Builders Pty. Ltd

turnOn, Austria
Architect: AllesWirdGut with Ingrid Hora
Website: www.alleswirdgut.cc
Project Team: AllesWirdGut, Ronald Zechner

Woodland cabin, southern Flanders, Belgium
Architect: Robbrecht en Daem Architecten
Website: www.robbrechtendaem.com
Project Team: Paul Robbrecht, Hilde Daem (principals), Cathérine Fierens
Landscape Architect: Herman Seghers

XS House, USA
Architect: Jay Shafer
Website: www.tumbleweedhouses.com
Project Team: Jenny Thomas, Pi Neuburg, Greg Johnson, Mat show (builders)
Client and main builder: Jay Shafer

INDEX

PICTURE CREDITS

169 Kristien Daem
170 NTPL/Matthew Antrobus
171 Courtesy Ortner & Ortner
172 l Dustin Feider
172r Courtesy Hofman Dujardin Architecten
173 Courtesy Sabina Lang and Daniel Baumann
175–179 Peter Bastianelli Kerze
181 'Castor'
183–185 Kilian O'Sullivan/lightroom
187–189 Steven Wooster
191–193 Dan Redmond
195–197 Courtesy eightyseven
199 Amir Sanei
201 Courtesy Carlosmartinez Architekten
203 Courtesy WILLIAMSONWILLIAMSON
205, 206, 207c Courtesy Tom Chudleigh
207t&b Alan Schroder
209–211 Patricia Meneses
213 Xavier Luchesi

Laurence King Publishing Ltd have paid DACS'
visual creators for the use of their artistic works.

AUTHOR'S ACKNOWLEDGEMENTS

The first acknowledgement must go to the architect Richard Horden, who invented the term 'microarchitecture' and who has been inspirational both through his elegantly realised projects and through his writings, which informed much of the introduction to this book.

Neither could the book have been written without the talent and imagination of all the other architects whose projects are shown here, and their cooperation in supplying information and images. Rich sources for discovering microarchitecture include the Small Projects issues of *The Architects' Journal* for work largely in the UK, and the Emerging Architecture issues of *The Architectural Review* for international schemes. There is also a host of websites on which this work appears, with www.mocoloco.com and www.treehugger.com as particular favourites.

I would like to thank friends and colleagues who have all in their own ways absorbed some of the stress and strain that comes from writing a book alongside a full-time and demanding job. In particular I should thank Isabel Allen and Sutherland Lyall for absorbing a certain amount of ranting when everything did not go exactly to plan, and Sutherland also gets thanks for his advice and support when I believed that my computer was dying irrevocably at key times.

Thanks as always and immeasurably to Barrie Evans for support, care, enthusiasm and reading every word.

I must thank my agent Shelley Power for ensuring that I bank my cheques eventually and those at Laurence King – Liz Faber, Jennifer Hudson, Philip Cooper, Kim Sinclair – and the designer, David Bothwell at Hybrid.

And, of course, thanks to anybody who has bought or borrowed the book, and has read this far.